SAYING KADDISH

OTHER BOOKS BY ANITA DIAMANT

NONFICTION

Choosing a Jewish Life
Bible Baby Names
The New Jewish Baby Book
Living a Jewish Life
The New Jewish Wedding

FICTION

The Red Tent

SAYING KADDISH

HOW TO COMFORT THE DYING, BURY THE DEAD, AND MOURN AS A JEW

ANITA DIAMANT

SCHOCKEN BOOKS
New York

Copyright © 1998 by Anita Diamant

All rights reserved under International and Pan-American
Copyright Conventions. Published in the United States by
Schocken Books Inc., New York, and simultaneously in Canada
by Random House of Canada Limited, Toronto. Distributed by
Pantheon Books, a division of Random House, Inc., New York.
SCHOCKEN and colophon are trademarks of
Schocken Books Inc.

Library of Congress Cataloging-in-Publication Data

Permissions Acknowledgments appear on pages 265–66.

Diamant, Anita.
Saying Kaddish : how to comfort the dying, bury the dead,
and mourn as a Jew / Anita Diamant.
p.   cm.
Includes bibliographical references and index.
ISBN 0-8052-4149-3
1. Jewish mourning customs.   2. Funeral rites and ceremonies,
Jewish.   3. Death—Religious aspects—Judaism.   4. Kaddish.
5. Judaism—Liturgy.   6. Consolation (Judaism)   I. Title.
BM712.D53   1998
296.4'45—dc21   98-16646
CIP

Random House Web Address: http://www.randomhouse.com/

Book design by Deborah Kerner

Printed in the United States of America
First Edition
2   4   6   8   9   7   5   3   1

For my brother
Harry Diamant

A BLESSING FOR MOURNERS

My brothers and sisters who are worn out and crushed by this mourning, let your hearts consider this:

This is the path that has existed from the time of creation and will exist forever. Many have drunk from it and many will yet drink. As was the first meal so shall be the last.

My brothers and sisters, may the One who comforts comfort you.

Blessed is the One who comforts the mourners.

A BLESSING FOR CONSOLERS

My brothers and sisters who perform acts of loving-kindness, children of those who perform acts of loving-kindness—who follow the way of our father Abraham and our mother Sarah.

My brothers and sisters may the One Who rewards goodness reward you.

Blessed is the One Who rewards deeds of goodness.[1]

V'imru, Amen.

CONTENTS

Contents

Contents

ACKNOWLEDGMENTS

My deepest thanks to the impossibly busy people who took the time to read and comment on early chapter drafts: David Browning, M.S.W., director of Safe Passage, a bereavement support program, Rabbi Barbara Penzner, Rabbi Carl Perkins, Rabbi David Wolfman. They are, each one, generous and wise, erudite and practical, patient and supportive friends and teachers: *todah rabbah*.

I am forever thanking Rabbi Lawrence Kushner, which is as it should be.

For their various contributions, including interviews, conversations, poetry, and permissions, thank you to Debra Cash, Howard Cooper, David Dechter, Lori Diamond, and Barbara Levine of Levine's Funeral Home in Brookline, Massachusetts, Miriam Drukman of the Jewish Cemetery Association of Massachusetts, Rabbi Amy Eilberg, Marcia Falk, Rabbi Nancy Flam, Professor Everett Fox, Robyn Greenberg, Rabbi Linda Holtzman, Rabbi Sharon Kleinbaum, Roberta Leviton, Rabbi Avis D. Miller, Edward Myers, Rebecca Newman, Danny Siegel, Cindy

Spittel of the Newton Memorial Art Company, Rabbi Moshe Waldoks, Arnie Zar-Kessler, Lorel Zar-Kessler, cantor at congregation Beth El of the Sudbury River Valley, and Rabbi Elaine Zecher.

My thanks to Arthur Samuelson and Jennifer Turvey at Schocken Books, for everything they did.

Writing a book about death and mourning is not easy. My husband and daughter were models of forbearance and support, my friends were patient and reassuring. Thank you all.

PREFACE

My father died a good death. He said good-bye to the people he loved and made his wishes known. His end was peaceful and dignified. Yet, even though I knew it was coming, the shock of his death was staggering. The world that I had known was gone and I would never be the same. A friend who lives above the San Andreas Fault in Los Angeles described the feeling as "a private earthquake."

During the days and weeks following my father's death, I explored the quiet devastation left by his loss. I assumed a new role and became a mourner. As lonely as I was without my dad, I was not alone. My family and my community comforted me, and I felt myself traveling down a path made smooth by centuries of Jewish mourners.

I chose to "sit *shiva*," staying at home for a week to fully experience the overwhelming first stage of grief. Friends, neighbors, and members of my synagogue came to the door, carrying food. I was hugged and kissed, stroked and patted, cared for in the most elemental ways. My rabbi sat with me at the kitchen table in the quiet of one afternoon. I reminisced about my father; he described the trajectory of grief.

Mostly, I remember very little of what people said to me. But the sound of their voices, their presence in my home, and the cards and notes that arrived in the mail, were all deeply consoling. As heavy as grief is, they bore me up.

On three of the evenings during my week of *shiva,* a prayer service led by members of my congregation was held in our living room. Before we recited the final prayer, the Kaddish, people spoke about my father. My husband and I shared memories of him. My then-nine-year-old daughter read a poem she'd written in his memory. The few of our friends who knew him told stories, too, and after a few minutes, people who had never met my father knew that he loved a good joke and lively conversation. His eternal optimism and faith in humanity brightened the room.

Then we said Kaddish: *Yit-ga-dal v'yit-ka-dash sh'mei ra-ba.*

I knew the words by heart from years of synagogue services, but the communal prayer was utterly transformed. Now it was a mantra of sadness and longing, a personal petition for peace and completion, an extended "Amen" to another exhausting day.

A candle burned in my house all that week in my father's memory. For the month after his death, his name was spoken in the synagogue at Sabbath services, where I was treated with special tenderness by strangers as well as friends.

In addition to notes and cards, the mail brought news of many tributes to my father, donations that reflected his values and beliefs. There were contributions to the memorial garden at my synagogue, gifts to the library at his temple, contributions to Amnesty International and to an organization that cares for righteous gentiles who rescued Jews during the Holocaust. I continue to make charitable contributions in his memory. I always will.

Every year, I light a memorial candle on the anniversary of his death. On Yom Kippur, I go to Yizkor, the memorial service, and stand with all the other mourners to listen for his name on the long, long list. And whenever I say Kaddish, I remember his smile, and it sustains me.

My father's death taught me the meaning of the word "blessing." His memory is a palpable blessing in my life, a reminder to stay in touch with beauty, to be kind, to laugh.

His death also taught me new lessons about the blessings of Jewish ritual and community. The structure of Jewish tradition (sitting *shiva*, setting the first month apart, attending services to say Kaddish, counting myself among the mourners) guided me through dark days. I explored new depths of connection to the synagogue where I had been a member for eighteen years. The outpouring of support and affection from members of Congregation Beth El of the Sudbury River Valley was due not simply to the presence of compassionate individuals in the congregation; the communal response to my loss was rooted in the ancient, holy requirement—the *mitzvah*—that Jews comfort the bereaved.

This book was hard to write. Philosophers and theologians have long recommended the contemplation of death as a way to stay in touch with the beauty of life. But contemplating death is so exhausting, I wonder whether human beings have an instinctive aversion to the subject. We cannot dwell too long on the idea that each of us will die, that all of us will grieve.

But grief is an inescapable condition of humanness—like the opposable thumb, like laughter. In this, we have no choice; if we live long enough, we are bound to lose people that we love. However, we do have a choice in how we grieve.

If you are reading these words looking for ways to help console a friend who is in mourning, I hope this book will help you in that sad but sacred task.

If you read these words while mourning the loss of someone you love, I hope that *Saying Kaddish* will enable you to make consoling choices in your grief. I hope that the Jewish practices described here will help you find solace and create meaning out of the chaos within and the chaos all around you.

I hope you have wonderful memories of the one who died, and that those memories will sustain you.

I pray that you find yourself in a community that will comfort you.

I pray you find peace as you continue on your way.

ANITA DIAMANT
Newton, Massachusetts
January 1998—Tevet 5758

SAYING KADDISH

INTRODUCTION

IN THE PAST, WHEN A JEW DIED, NO ONE ASKED, "WHEN should we schedule the funeral?" or "How much would you like to spend on a casket?" or "Where will she be buried?" Members of the *hevra kadisha*—the local volunteer burial society—simply appeared and began preparing the body for burial in the community cemetery at a funeral that was like all the other Jewish funerals.

The mourners knew what to do, too. They ripped their clothing and sat on the floor. They stayed home where prayer services were held three times a day until the first week of mourning was over. Heartbroken as mourners might be, they were not alone, since neighbors and friends would fill the house with food and sympathetic faces.

In other words, Jews learned how to bury the dead and how to comfort the bereaved simply by living their lives.

It doesn't work that way anymore. Jewish families are scattered and the community is dispersed. American Jews have, for several generations, lost touch with the context and continuities of their own mourning traditions, following secular burial customs and adopting secular attitudes about bereavement—including the larger culture's tendency to underestimate the power of grief and the impact of loss.

Death itself has become something of a stranger. In the past, life spans were shorter and the tragedy of infant mortality touched most families. People usually died at home, surrounded by loved ones, including children. Funerals, like weddings, were not invitational events, but community-wide gatherings.

But today, it is possible to reach the age of forty without ever attending a funeral or visiting a house of mourning. In addition to great advances in medical science, death and dying are removed from the flow of daily life. Despite the increased use of home-based hospice care, most people die in hospitals and nursing homes. Thus, death comes as a terrifying shock, leaving the bereaved unprepared and adrift. What do I do now?

Saying Kaddish answers that question for contemporary liberal Jews seeking answers from their own tradition. The totality of Jewish mourning customs and traditions, laws and practices, creates a temporary home for the bereft, a sanctuary for loss where healing is possible because weeping is not only permitted but encouraged.

Rabbi Abraham Joshua Heschel once described Jewish ritual as "the art of significant forms in time, as architecture of time,"[1] Jewish life-cycle customs and holidays can be thought of as "cathedrals" made of time.

The blueprint for the mourner's "cathedral" can be imagined as a series of concentric circles defined by the passage of the first week, the first month, the first year, and the anniversary of a death. The innermost circle is the darkest, but as the weeks pass, mourners move from the dimness of remembering and weeping to the light of rejoicing in the memory of life.

Traditional Jewish law, *halachah,* is very clear about this process, defining what is permitted and what is forbidden for the dying, the dead, and the bereaved. While there is great comfort in understanding the architecture of Jewish mourning customs, this knowledge is only the beginning for non-Orthodox Jews— Conservative, Reconstructionist, Reform, and unaffiliated—who tend to view *halachah* as reference point and guide rather than mandate.[2] Liberal Jews committed to burying and mourning their dead within a clearly Jewish framework often face questions and choices that are outside the purview of the law.

- Will we be sitting *shiva*? For how long?
- What do we do with flowers sent to the funeral home?
- If Dad never wore a prayer shawl, would it be disrespectful to him to have his body wrapped in one for burial?

Contemporary life brings heartfelt new questions to the universal crisis of grief:

- How can I, as a Jew-by-choice, mourn for my Catholic father or my Baptist sister?
- How do I reconcile the fact that Mom told us she wanted to be cremated when Judaism opposes it?
- Since virtually all Jewish mourning rituals pertain to first-degree family members, how can I grieve for my best friend?
- How do I mourn for a lover?
- How do I mourn my ex-husband, who was the father of my children?

- Is it hypocritical to recite Kaddish if I don't believe in God?

There are no one-size-fits-all answers to such questions. As in all aspects of Jewish life, there is enormous variation in the way that Jews bury and mourn their loved ones. Every rabbi and synagogue has a distinctive set of customs, or *minhagim*. There are even geographic differences, with the Jews of one city following certain customs that seem strange in another.

Even so, there is remarkable unanimity in the principles that underlie this diversity. Every Jewish ritual and custom that surrounds death is guided by two *mitzvot*, two primary commandments: the requirement to show respect for the dead—*kevod ha-met*—and the commandment to provide comfort for the bereaved—*nichum avelim*. No matter how differently they are elaborated, these are the dual cornerstones of the Jewish approach to death and mourning, and the organizing principle of *Saying Kaddish*. The goal of this book is to help you express these *mitzvot* in your own way.

Part I, "Why We Say Kaddish," explains why this short prayer remains such a powerful religious, cultural, and communal part of Jewish life. Kaddish (literally "sanctified," from the same root as *kadosh*, or holy) is recited in memory of loved ones who have died. Chapter 1 describes the power of the ancient Aramaic prayer, which transcends language, and also explores the meaning of its words, line by line. Chapter 2 places Kaddish in its liturgical and historical context.

Part II, "Respect for the Dying, Respect for the Dead" focuses on how Jews deal with the reality of death, from the sickroom until the end of the funeral. Chapter 3 describes the Jewish approach to end-of-life issues, including how to speak to the dying, and the Jewish deathbed confession called Viddui. Chapter 4 explains the *mitzvah* of *kevod ha-met,* honoring the body, including traditional ways of preparing it for burial, shrouds, and choosing a coffin. Chapter 5 provides a full description of Jewish funerals, the centerpiece of which is the eulogy.

In Part III: "Compassion for the Bereaved," the attention shifts from the care of the dead to caring for the living. Chapter 6, "The Landscape of Mourning," describes grief in its various shapes, forms, and dimensions, from the physical to the familial to the theological; it also provides information about how to find support and good advice in a difficult time.

Chapters 7 and 8 lay out the architecture of Jewish mourning. "Shiva" details the seven-day period after the funeral. "The First Year" begins with *shloshim,* a transitional month when the mourner is protected from the world even as he or she is encouraged to return to it, and ends with the *yahrzeit,* the anniversary of a death.

Chapter 9, "The Consolations of Memory," describes the custom of unveiling the tombstone, the Yizkor prayer, and Jewish traditions about visiting a grave. This chapter also explains the role of prayer and charity in translating grief into healing.

Chapter 10, "Particular Losses," raises some difficult issues in mourning, including bereaved children, mourning for non-Jewish loved ones, neonatal loss, and suicide.

Part IV, "Eight More Ways to Say Kaddish," is a collection of translations, interpretations, and poetic reflections on the prayer, for use by mourners and comforters.

There is comfort to be found in the pages of *Saying Kaddish,* but no book can provide the kind of solace every mourner deserves. For that, you need to feel the embrace of family and friends. You need to hear an honest eulogy that makes you cry. You need to share your memories. You need other people.

Although grief is an intensely personal emotion, Judaism treats this time of life as it does all others, insisting, "It is not good to be alone."[3] Just as Jewish law and custom mandates marriage and discourages hermits, and prefers the give-and-take of group discussion over solitary study, Jewish mourners are thrust into the center of their communities. Thus, in order to say Kaddish—which is the central religious gesture of Jewish bereavement—mourners must stand with at least nine other Jews.

Every Jewish mourner follows the path of all the Jewish mourners who proceeded him or her. When you rise to say Kaddish, you are shoulder-to-shoulder with everyone who stands or ever stood as you do, recalling a beloved face that is gone but not forgotten. The traditional prayer of condolence acknowledges this larger Jewish community: "May the Holy One[4] comfort you among all the mourners of Zion and Jerusalem."

This is a gathering that transcends time and place.

Truly, you are not alone.

PART I

WHY WE SAY
KADDISH

THE MOURNER'S KADDISH

יִתְגַּדַּל וְיִתְקַדַּשׁ שְׁמֵהּ רַבָּא בְּעָלְמָא דִּי בְרָא כִרְעוּתֵהּ
וְיַמְלִיךְ מַלְכוּתֵהּ בְּחַיֵּיכוֹן וּבְיוֹמֵיכוֹן וּבְחַיֵּי דְכָל בֵּית
יִשְׂרָאֵל בַּעֲגָלָא וּבִזְמַן קָרִיב וְאִמְרוּ אָמֵן:
יְהֵא שְׁמֵהּ רַבָּא מְבָרַךְ לְעָלַם וּלְעָלְמֵי עָלְמַיָּא:
יִתְבָּרַךְ וְיִשְׁתַּבַּח וְיִתְפָּאַר וְיִתְרוֹמַם וְיִתְנַשֵּׂא וְיִתְהַדָּר
וְיִתְעַלֶּה וְיִתְהַלָּל שְׁמֵהּ דְּקֻדְשָׁא בְּרִיךְ הוּא
לְעֵלָּא (לְעֵלָּא) מִן כָּל בִּרְכָתָא וְשִׁירָתָא תֻּשְׁבְּחָתָא וְנֶחֱמָתָא
דַּאֲמִירָן בְּעָלְמָא וְאִמְרוּ אָמֵן:
יְהֵא שְׁלָמָא רַבָּא מִן שְׁמַיָּא וְחַיִּים עָלֵינוּ וְעַל כָּל
יִשְׂרָאֵל וְאִמְרוּ אָמֵן:
עוֹשֶׂה שָׁלוֹם בִּמְרוֹמָיו הוּא יַעֲשֶׂה שָׁלוֹם עָלֵינוּ וְעַל
כָּל יִשְׂרָאֵל וְאִמְרוּ אָמֵן:

Yit-ga-dal ve'yit-ka-dash sh'mei ra-ba

B'alma di-ve-ra chir-u-tei v'yam-lich mal-chu-tei
b'chai-yei chon u-v-yo-mei-chon
u-v'chai-yei d'chol beit yis-ra-el
ba-a-ga-la u-viz-man ka-riv
v'im-ru amen.

Y'hei shmei ra-ba m'va-rach
l'a-lam u-l'al-mei al-mai-ya
Yit-ba-rach v'yish-ta-bach
v'yit-pa-ar v'yit-ro-mam v'yit-na-sei

v'yit-ha-dar v'yit-a-leh v'yit-ha-lal
sh'mei d'ku-d'sha b'rich hu

l'ei-lah min kol bir-cha-ta v'shi-ra-ta
tush-b'cha-ta v'neh-cheh-ma-ta
da-a-mi-ran b'al-ma
v'im-ru amen

Y'hei shla-ma ra-ba min sh'ma-ya
V'cha-yim a-lei-nu
v'al kol yis-ra-el
v'im-ru amen

O-seh sha-lom bim-ro-mav hu ya-a-seh sha-lom
a-lei-nu v'al kol yis-ra-el
V'im ru, Amen.

Exalted and hallowed be God's greatness
In this world of Your creation.
May Your will be fulfilled
And Your sovereignty revealed
And the life of the whole house of Israel
Speedily and soon.
And say, Amen.

May You be blessed forever,
Even to all eternity.
May You, most Holy One, be blessed,
Praised and honored, extolled and glorified,
Adored and exalted above all else.

Blessed are You.
Beyond all blessings and hymns, praises and consolations
That may be uttered in this world,

In the days of our lifetime,
And say, Amen.

May peace abundant descend from heaven
With life for us and for all Israel,
And say, Amen.

May God, Who makes peace on high,
Bring peace to all and to all Israel,
And say, Amen.

KADDISH IS A MYSTERY.

It sounds like comfort and feels like a transcendent embrace, and yet, the prayer that is synonymous with Jewish mourning does not mention death or consolation. It does not speak of loss, sadness, or bereavement. Nor is there anything about life after death in these brief lines, which seem to echo with loss and longing.

For most Jews, the literal meaning of Kaddish is either opaque or troubling. "Kaddish" means "holy" and the prayer is a doxology—a listing of God's holy attributes. "Blessed, praised and honored, extolled and glorified, adored and exalted."

These are hard words for most mourners. After all, this is the same God who ordained or permitted the death of a loved one. And yet, for centuries Jewish tradition has placed this prayer in the mouths of people who have no taste for praise.

Jewish mourners begin saying Kaddish at the funerals of their loved ones, and continue reciting it for the rest of their lives. Jews who never pray say Kaddish. Atheists say Kaddish.

As inconsistent as it may seem, this does not offend Jewish religious sensibilities. Judaism has always been far less concerned with belief than with action or *mitzvah*, which means "commandment" or "sacred obligation." The tradition mandates saying Kaddish, with clear directions about how, where, and when it should be said. But *halachah*, or Jewish law, does not require belief in the words—or even understanding. It is enough that the mourner just "do the *mitzvah*" of saying the prayer with nine other Jews. Which is why Kaddish is always transliterated, so that everyone can participate, regardless of whether they can read the Hebrew letters or know what they are saying.

This is not as mechanical as it sounds, because it is simply impossible to understand the impact or value of saying Kaddish without first doing it. The mystery of Kaddish is revealed every time it is spoken aloud with others. The truth is that the sounds of the words are more important than their definitions. The text is secondary to the emotional experience of its recitation. The meaning only comes clear when given communal voice.

Even so, the words are not insignificant. Kaddish addresses the meaning of life and death, immortality and redemption, the purpose and efficacy of prayer, community, and the ultimate goal of peace. It even speaks—in its silence—about the predominant Jewish view of the afterlife.

But the language of the prayer is not transparent. Kaddish requires that the mourner wrestle with the text. Through study and thought, reading and discussion, Kaddish demands that the mourner engage, connect, and forge a personal connection to it. Although these words have been studied and analyzed for centuries, every mourner finds new meaning in them, year by year, and line by line.

But the bottom line is startlingly clear. In words and through practice, Kaddish insists that the mourner turn away from death and choose life.

In this way, Kaddish expresses the essence of Judaism. The rest is commentary.

....

CHAPTER ONE

WHAT KADDISH MEANS

Beyond language, Kaddish is more than the sum of its words. First and foremost, it is an experience of the senses. Like music, there is no understanding Kaddish without hearing and feeling it and letting go of the words.

One of the great ironies of Kaddish is that it was written in a vernacular language so that it could be understood and led by scholars and laborers alike. Today, of course, Aramaic is far more obscure than Hebrew.

That the recitation of words long dead can remain a source of consolation testifies to the fact that Kaddish transcends language. Its comforts are rooted in preverbal ways of knowing. Like a mother's heartbeat against the infant ear, Kaddish makes an elemental sound—natural as rain on a wooden roof and as human as a lullaby.

In addition to being a profession of faith and a doxology, it is also mantra and meditation. In rhythmic repetition of syllables and sounds, the list of praises (glorified, celebrated, lauded) builds into a kind of incantation:

Yit-ba-rach v'yish-ta-bach
v'yit-pa-ar v'yit-ro-mam v'yit-na-sei
v'yit-ha-dar v'yit-a-leh v'yit-ha-lal
sh'mei d'ku-d'sha b'rich hu
l'ei-lah min kol bir-cha-ta v'shi-ra-ta
tush-b'cha-ta v'neh-cheh-ma-ta
da-a-mi-ran b'al-ma, v'im-ru amen

On some level, the words are pretext. The real meaning, the subtext, is embedded in the repetition of "yit" and "ah," in consonants and vowels. Kaddish whispers "Amen, Amen" like a parent who murmurs "Hush, hush."

Kaddish is an essentially aural experience—perhaps another reason the rabbis were so insistent it be recited within a *minyan*. Only with a collective voice is there enough energy to lift up the lonely mourner, the angry mourner, the mourner too hurt to even say "Amen." The *minyan* chorus implicitly reassures the wounded soul, "You are not alone."

Syllable by syllable, shoulder-to-shoulder, Kaddish is a sigh that affirms the core beliefs and dreams of the Jewish people: God is beyond us. Understanding is beyond us. Holiness and beauty are all around us, but beyond us, too. We have work to do. There is hope. Peace is possible.

Peace. Please. Peace.

KADDISH—WORD BY WORD: Even though the words are secondary, they are not incidental. Kaddish is a love song to God, praising the Holy One in a myriad of ways. Although extolling God sounds as though it should be a joyful activity, the Hebrew word for worship, *avodah*, also means work, and perhaps no act of worship requires more effort than one that asks mourners to praise God.

The death of a loved one—especially an untimely death—confronts even the most faithful Jew with doubt. The bereaved mother of a five-year-old child is supposed to stand and "magnify and sanctify" alongside a seventy-year-old son who has lost a ninety-year-old mother.

Exalted and hallowed be God's greatness
In this world of Your creation.

In the mouth of the mourner, these words affirm that even death is part of God's creation. Kaddish asks Jews to hallow death—to take what might appear random, meaningless, and cruel, and speak of it as part of the sacred whole. This is an enormous challenge—perhaps even a lifelong struggle. Many view it as a goal.

Kaddish also pronounces acceptance of God's judgment. There is no lamentation and certainly no argument in the prayer, which recalls Job's response to all the terrible things that befell him. In the ultimate statement of acceptance, Job said, "Though God slay me, yet will I trust in God."[1]

That was Job. The rest of humanity finds it harder to trust God completely in the face of loss and suffering. Even so, all human beings must ultimately accept death. There is finally no way to answer to "Why him?" "Why now?" Acceptance is a refuge from insanity; a way to find surcease of pain even when there is no way to make sense of the loss.

Nevertheless, mourners are not expected to provide the final affirmation that is "Amen." When Kaddish is given its traditional call-and-response reading,[2] the mourner says *"v'im-ru,"* which means "and you should say." The bereaved thus elicit an "Amen" from the community that rallies around mourners for just this purpose. The "Amen" that comes from a mourner's mouth is spoken with quotation marks around it.

And Your sovereignty revealed
In the days of our lifetime
And the life of the whole house of Israel
Speedily and soon.

Although Kaddish gives voice to acceptance, it is not a statement of submission. In a way, it is a petitionary prayer. It seeks nothing less than the redemption of the whole world—the perfection of God's creation. And not in the sweet by-and-by either, but soon, "in the days of our lifetime."

The request for revelation of God's "sovereignty" speaks to the timeless hope for the day when justice will prevail and all people will live in peace. For most Jews, this vision of the end of days, of a messianic time, depends upon human action rather than divine intervention. By doing what God asks—working for peace and justice, performing *mitzvot*—human beings can bring about the kingdom of heaven on earth. Kaddish reminds mourners of their obligation both to dream of such a world and to build it—without delay.

This is not an easy message to hear or accept when your world has been shattered. Still, Kaddish is given to mourners precisely because they are most aware of the fragility of life. The bereaved know better than anyone that there is no time to waste in making God's presence manifest in the world, both in praising God's name and in the work of repairing the world.[3]

May You be blessed forever,
Even to all eternity.
May You, most Holy One, be blessed,
Praised and honored, extolled and glorified,
Adored and exalted above all else.

Blessed are You.
Beyond all blessings and hymns, praises and consolations
That may be uttered in this world . . .

This long list of attributes—counted by various authorities as seven, ten, or even fifteen[4]—points to God's inscrutability and humanity's inability to describe the Holy One, regardless of how many praises we heap up.

The words have been given many translations: glorified and celebrated, lauded and praised, acclaimed and honored, extolled and exalted, blessed, upraised, elevated. This is followed by another series, again variously translated as songs, praises, psalms, consolations, blessings, hymns.

Kaddish puts this accumulation of affirmation into the mourner's mouth, maintaining the connection, however tenuous, between the bereaved and the Holy One. Someday, when the bereaved can once again taste the food on his plate and delight in the birdsong outside her window, these praises may no longer seem like an affront. Having recited Kaddish during their residence in the valley of the shadow, there need be no shame for having doubted or even cursed God's name in that dark place.

May peace abundant descend from heaven
With life for us and for all Israel . . .

May God, Who makes peace on high,
Bring peace to us and to all Israel.

Kaddish ends with a fervent double plea for peace, first in Aramaic and then, with nearly the same words, in Hebrew. "*Oseh shalom bim-romav*" comes from a line found in the Book of Job, where tragedy is ultimately transformed into a hard-won blessing.

The repetition of *shalom,* the most familiar of all Hebrew words, echoes like a promise of peace after the petition for peace. There are many kinds of peace. Kaddish speaks to both inner peace and to the peace of the whole world. And because of the connection between Kaddish and the ties that bind families together, it is also very much about *shalom bayit*—peace within the home, within the family.

Every death leaves unfinished family business; saying Kaddish in memory of a loved one is one way that mourners forgive the dead and themselves for words spoken in anger and for words of love and forgiveness never given voice. Kaddish helps replace grudges and guilt with *shalom*—peace for the mourner, peace among the mourners, peace for all the mourners of Zion.

AFTERLIFE: There is no mention of heaven in the Kaddish. Even though it is recited "in honor of" the dead, and in spite of the fact that for centuries Jews thought of saying Kaddish as a way of "redeeming" parents from hell (explained in Chapter 2, in the section "In History"), the afterlife is conspicuously absent. This silence not only begs the question about what Jews believe about life after death, it provides an answer, too.

There is not now, nor has there ever been, one unified doctrinal Jewish view of the afterlife. Jews have embraced the gamut

of beliefs about what happens to human beings after they die—
from simple decomposition to reincarnation, from elaborate
depictions of heaven and hell to humanistic metaphors about the
biological legacy of children and the tangible-spiritual legacy of
good works.[5]

Maimonides, the influential twelfth-century rabbinic inter-
preter, affirmed belief in an afterlife but viewed the topic as
utterly beyond human comprehension, and thus best left alone:
"As to the blissful state of the soul in the World to Come, there is
no way on earth in which we can comprehend or know it."[6] In
the twentieth century, the overwhelming atrocity of the Holocaust nearly obliterated the idea of a personal afterlife, and yet
also renewed the ancient idea of a collective immortality within
the communal entity of the Jewish people.

The reticence of Kaddish about the afterlife leaves room for
the great variety of Jewish belief about the world to come (*ha-
olam ha-bah*). But it also reflects Judaism's commitment to the
primacy of life in this world (*ha-olam ha-zeh*). In marked contrast to Christian funerals, which usually mention a reward in
heaven or reunion with God and/or loved ones, the Jewish
funeral liturgy never speaks of death as a "better place."

Jewish funerals focus almost exclusively on the life that was
lived and is now lost. Indeed, it is incumbent upon the person
delivering the eulogy—the centerpiece of the funeral—to extol
what was praiseworthy about the deceased—just as the Kaddish
extols God.

Judaism's relative indifference to the afterlife is apparent in
the laws and customs that surround death. Mourners and consol-
ers are not encouraged to reflect upon a loved one's life after
death; instead, they are given practical ways to focus upon their
responsibilities in this world, with laws and customs about how

to show respect toward the dying and the dead, how to grieve, and how to comfort the bereaved. These *mitzvot*—or commandments—are the subject of the rest of this book.

Saying Kaddish is a *mitzvah,* too, and one that, like giving charity in honor of a loved one, has the remarkable ability to transform the ineffable memory of the dead into tangible action and perhaps into something more.

"Love is strong as death," says the poet in the Song of Songs. From generation to generation, saying Kaddish demonstrates the immortality of love.

CHAPTER TWO

....

KADDISH
IN PRACTICE

It is hard to overstate the importance of Kaddish within the liturgy; it is part of virtually all communal Jewish worship. Indeed, because the sanctification of God's name is considered one of the primary functions of Jewish worship, Kaddish has been called a "self-contained miniature service."[1]

It is also hard to overstate the power of saying Kaddish with other people. Jewish law mandates that the sanctification of God's name always requires ten voices, implying that fewer cannot do justice to such an awesome task. The requirement of a *minyan* for Kaddish also turns the prayer into a communalizing force, keeping the mourner among the living—both literally and metaphorically. Indeed, the power of Kaddish comes, in large measure, from the consolations of being in a group that recognizes and embraces the bereaved.

Who Says Kaddish: According to Jewish law, anyone who has lost a parent, sibling, child, or spouse recites Kaddish every day, beginning with the funeral and continuing for thirty days after the death. When a parent dies, children are obliged to continue saying Kaddish for eleven or twelve months.

Many people choose to say Kaddish for people outside their immediate nuclear family. Bereaved parents, spouses, and siblings often say it for a whole year rather than just the required month of *shloshim*. Friends and lovers do, too. The tradition does not prohibit anyone from widening the circle. (Chapters 7 and 8 contain more about the choices, customs, and social dimensions of saying Kaddish during the first year of mourning.)

WHEN AND WHERE: Kaddish can be recited in any place, and Jewish tradition provides mourners with a myriad of opportunities to say the prayer. Virtually every synagogue service includes a Kaddish, and study groups of ten or more sometimes conclude with it as well.

According to *halachah*, Kaddish is forbidden in the absence of community; a Jew who cannot get to a *minyan* is told to study the weekly Torah portion or read from the Prophets instead; those who are able are encouraged to study Mishnah or a page from the Talmud. Nonetheless, the sound and rhythm of this prayer are so deeply embedded in Jewish hearts and souls, some contemporary liberal Jews do read or recite the Kaddish as a private meditation, and find comfort in it.

IN THE SYNAGOGUE: Kaddish is recited on Shabbat and on weekdays, at morning and evening services, on fast days and joyful holidays.[2] It is repeated like a liturgical "comma" between sections of the service, and at the end as a solemn coda after *Alenu*. In some traditional congregations, it is recited as many as thirteen times in a single service.

There are actually five versions of the Kaddish, which vary by only a few lines. All forms begin with the same clarion words: *Yit-ga-dal ve'yit-ka-dash sh'mei ra-ba*—"Exalted and hallowed be God's greatness." All but the Burial Kaddish share the same two opening paragraphs.

The Burial Kaddish is recited only after closing a grave. After sanctifying God's name, it asks for a restored Temple in Jerusalem and for the day when the dead will be revived and raised, two articles of faith that are difficult for many contemporary Jews. Though normative at Orthodox funerals, liberal Jews almost always substitute the better-known Mourner's Kaddish.[3]

The Rabbi's Kaddish (*Kaddish DeRabbanan*) seeks additional blessings upon teachers and sages. It is recited after a learned discourse, sermon, or after studying a Jewish text when there is a *minyan*. In some prayer books, *Kaddish DeRabbanan* is found in the *shacharit* (morning) service and at the end, before *Alenu*.[4]

Kaddish Shalem is the "full" Kaddish. Recited by the prayer leader at the end of a major portion of a worship service, it is also called *Kaddish Titkabel* because it includes a line that starts with the word *titkabel*—"let it be accepted." This version is the same as the Rabbi's Kaddish except for the addition of this verse, which asks God to accept all the prayers that were recited: "Let the prayers and supplications of all Israel be accepted by our God in Heaven, and say Amen."

The Chatzi (Partial) Kaddish contains all but the last two lines of the mourner's version of the prayer. This form is used to "punctuate" the worship service, delineating where one part ends and another begins. During the morning service, for example, the *Chatzi Kaddish* is recited after psalms and before the *Barchu*, the call to worship.[5]

The Mourner's Kaddish is the most familiar version, the one that is meant by the phrase, "saying Kaddish." Every prayer book provides a transliteration of this form, so that people who cannot read the Hebrew letters can utter the words and have the honor of leading their congregation.

The Mourner's Kaddish is said after burial at liberal funerals, at Yizkor, on *yahrzeits*, and at virtually all worship services.[6] In some congregations, it follows *Kaddish Shalem*, which is recited by the prayer leader. The Mourner's Kaddish is then recited by people who have lost a loved one within the past month or year; the congregation joins them in the "Amens."

THE "CHOREOGRAPHY" OF THE MOURNER'S KADDISH: The prayer is always read standing. However, there are significant variations among synagogues about exactly who stands for the prayer.

Usually, before recitation of the Mourner's Kaddish, the rabbi or prayer leader reads the names of temple members who have died, temple members who have become bereaved in the past month, and a list of names of people for whom a memorial Kaddish (*yahrzeit*) is being said that week in the congregation.

In many Conservative temples, only mourners rise for the Mourner's Kaddish. This focuses attention on the recently bereaved so that the community can offer condolences later.

In many Reform temples, the custom is for everyone present to rise for Kaddish. This custom spares recently bereaved people who may feel too fragile to accept condolences from strangers; it also prevents embarrassment if a name is read aloud and no family member is present. After the Holocaust, the Reform movement decided that its congregations would say Kaddish for the 6 million Jewish victims of the Nazis.

Some liberal congregations combine these two impulses—for

individual acknowledgment and communal solidarity. Sometimes family members stand as the names of their loved ones are read aloud; then the entire congregation stands with them to say Kaddish. Alternatively, after everyone rises for Kaddish, the rabbi reads a list of names of those who died in the last week or month and then invites others who have come to observe a *yahrzeit* to name their loved one, too.

IN HISTORY: Beloved from its earliest days, parts of the Kaddish date from the first century B.C.E. Written mostly in Aramaic—the spoken language of most Jews from the fifth century B.C.E. until the fifth century C.E.—it was recited not only by priests, but by common folk as well.

The Lord's Prayer, or Pater Noster, is the Christian analog to the Kaddish. Based on verses from the Gospel of Matthew (6:9–13), it was written around the same time. Both prayers extol God's strength and ask for the establishment of God's sovereignty on earth. The Kaddish and the Lord's Prayer are also used in much the same ways: recited at most services and at virtually all funerals, they bind their respective faith communities with universally familiar words and rhythms.

Kaddish originated not in the synagogue but in the house of study (*bet midrash*). After a scholar delivered a learned discourse, students and teachers would rise to praise God's name. During the mourning period for a rabbi, or teacher, students would gather to study in his honor, and his son was given the honor of leading the prayer. Over time, reciting Kaddish replaced studying as the tribute given to a scholar. Eventually the custom extended to all mourners—not only the survivors of rabbis and leaders. By the sixth century, Kaddish was part of synagogue prayers,[7] and during the thirteenth century, when the Crusades threatened the Jewish communities of Europe, it became inextricably linked to loss and mourning.

Familiar, accessible, and comforting, Kaddish became part of the folk religion of the Jews. There are many Talmudic stories about the value of having the whole community recite the key words: "May His great name be blessed."

One of the better-known tales is attributed to Rabbi Akiva, who came across a man suffering terrible torments in hell. The rabbi found the poor man's long-lost son and taught him to recite the verse, "May His great name be blessed." With those words, the father's soul was released and flew up to heaven.[8]

For centuries, people believed that saying Kaddish would shorten the amount of time the deceased spent in Gehenna (hell) before ascending to Gan Eden (heaven).[9] Sons were referred to as "my Kaddish" or as a "*Kaddishl*," and people who had no sons sometimes hired men to say the prayer after they died.

Rabbinic authorities argued against this quid pro quo view of prayer. A sixteenth-century rabbi, Abraham Hurwitz, wrote, "Let the son keep a particular precept given him by his father, and it shall be of greater worth than the recital of the Kaddish. The same is true also of daughters."[10]

In twentieth-century America, the word Kaddish—like *shiva* and *shalom*—has found its way into the popular lexicon. Allen Ginsberg's 1959 poem "Kaddish" introduced it to a largely non-Jewish literary audience. While it shocked some Jews with its juxtaposition of profanity and the range of emotions associated with the loss of a parent, it was also a stunning affirmation of Jewishness during an era when most Jews wanted nothing more than to blend into the secular landscape.

Thirty-five years later, audiences heard the entire Kaddish

during performances of Tony Kushner's Pulitzer Prize–winning play *Angels in America*. Once again, there was an element of shock as an openly gay man said the traditional words over the body of a closeted gay man. But by that point in history, this artifact of Jewishness was considered so commonplace that the playwright even made a joke confusing Kaddish with Kiddush (the prayer recited over wine). The assumption that the audience was Jewishly sophisticated enough to "get it" was not at all unreasonable, given that television had already acquainted a mass audience with the prayer.[11]

WOMEN AND KADDISH: According to Jewish law, women are excused from the obligation to perform what are called positive or time-bound *mitzvot*. Among these are attendance at daily prayer services and saying Kaddish for the dead. The traditional explanation for the exemption from public duties is that the work of mothers and wives was too vital to be interrupted.

However, the exemption from saying Kaddish has long felt exclusionary and even punitive to many Jewish women. In 1916, when Henrietta Szold, the founder of the Zionist women's organization Hadassah, lost her mother, Szold refused a male friend's offer to say Kaddish. Her letter to him is a classic statement of Jewish women's self-empowerment.

"I believe that the elimination of women from such duties was never intended by our law and custom—women were free from positive duties when they could not perform them, but not when they could. It was never intended that, if they could perform them, their performance of them should not be considered as valuable and valid as when one of the male sex performed them. And of the Kaddish I feel sure this is particularly true. When my father died, my mother would not permit others to take her daughters' place in saying the Kaddish, and so I am sure I am acting in her spirit when I am moved to decline your offer."[12]

Now that women are full members of the minyan—the prayer quorum of ten—in all liberal congregations, women routinely say Kaddish for their loved ones.[13] But even though it is perfectly commonplace, reciting the prayer still feels like a watershed for many women, moving them from observer to participant, from outsider to insider.[14]

PART II

RESPECT FOR THE DYING, RESPECT FOR THE DEAD

....

CHAPTER THREE

CARE
OF THE DYING

TO SIT AT THE BEDSIDE OF A LOVED ONE WHO IS DYING IS to know profound powerlessness. And yet, even after there is nothing left to "do for" him, there is still the responsibility—and the opportunity—to "be with" him. Professional pastoral care-givers call this "the ministry of presence." In Hebrew, it is known as *bikkur holim*, visiting the sick, and while this is part of the pastoral duties of pulpit rabbis, it is also a *mitzvah*—a sacred responsibility—incumbent upon all Jews.

The *mitzvah* of *bikkur holim*, of being present, is not just a matter of sitting or standing in the same room as a sick or dying person, but of being attentive to the whole person in the bed and not just to symptoms. This kind of presence is no small thing, since a lonely death is one of the most fearful prospects on earth. In the end, being present is both the only thing and the greatest thing we have to give one another.

Jewish law is adamant about treating the dying person with the same respect due any living person. A person who is very close to death is called a *gosses* (goe-*sace*) and is to be provided with every comfort available. A *gosses* is still fully a member of the community; someone who can be counted for a *minyan,* serve as a witness, or even sit on a judicial tribunal—a *bet din.* The Talmud is emphatic on this point: "A dying person is to be considered a living person in all matters of the world."[1]

An ethical boundary is constructed around people in their last days to keep them from being treated only as patients, or even worse, as corpses-in-waiting. It is forbidden to start mourning until after the moment of death. Before death, "We do not rend the garments, bare the shoulder, deliver a memorial address, or bring the coffin into the house."[2]

But the prohibition goes beyond simply getting ready for the funeral; it requires that caregivers be attentive to what they say and do in the presence of a dying person, regardless of his or her medical condition. Standing at the bedside and talking about the person in the bed as though she were not present—even if she is in a deep coma—shows terrible disrespect. Similarly, talking about a terminally ill person in the past tense annihilates him. "Whoever closes the eyes of a *gosses* is considered as if he has taken a life."[3]

The mandate at the deathbed is to be fully present, attentive, and responsive. Although you may be unable to do what you most wish (make your loved one better, buy more time, change the course of the illness), there may still be many things you can do:

Listen: If your loved one wants to tell stories from her past, listen with a hearing heart. Life review is sometimes a person's final "work," their last effort at creating and finding meaning. Sharing stories can be a crowning gift.

Follow: Always let the dying person take the lead. If he does *not* wish to reminisce about his past, don't insist. If he wants to talk about death, don't change the subject. By the same token, if he refuses to discuss his own demise, it is not your place to confront him with it. If possible, do what he asks. For example, if he insists that you leave the hospital to rest, obeying is a way of returning a sense of agency to him.

Accept: People tend to die as they lived. Bitter people die in bitterness. The sweet-natured die more easily. Deathbed transformations, though not unheard of, are rare. Respect for the dying requires letting them be who they are, and accepting them unconditionally.

Speak: It is said that hearing is the last of the senses to go. If your loved one is willing to listen, or even if she is beyond responding, give voice to your feelings. Talk about memories that you cherish and that will stay with you. Apologize for any unkind words or misunderstandings between you. Forgive her for any unkindness she might have done to you.

Read aloud from a book that has meaning for your loved one or for you. Pray, if you are comfortable with praying. Sing, if you are moved to sing.

Touch: It is the most elemental form of presence and communication. Even if you were not physically affectionate before a final illness, holding his hand or placing your hand on a shoulder or arm provides physical reassurance that he is not alone and that his end will not be lonely.

Care for yourself: You cannot care for a loved one if you neglect your own health and well-being. Especially in cases of lingering final illness, caregivers must remember their own needs for food, rest, and respite. Remember that you cannot give your all to someone else when your own resources are depleted.

Reassure: Sometimes dying people will hold on to life, even in misery, because of fear for their loved ones. Offer reassurance that, as much as you will miss her, you and the rest of the family will be all right. That her life will be remembered and treasured. That her memory will sustain you.

Some caregivers refuse to leave the bedside for fear that death will come while they are gone. But dying people, wishing to protect the ones they love, may find it difficult to let go while others are in the room. If you have said everything that needed to be said, if you have been present and attentive, there is no need for self-recrimination. Your love does not vanish when you leave the room.

PRAYER AT THE BEDSIDE: If your loved one and/or your family never prayed or discussed religion or spiritual matters before a final illness, it's unlikely that this will change, even at the deathbed. However, in some cases, "business as usual" is set aside as death approaches.

It is quite common for people to express religious or spiritual longings at the end of life, or when facing the death of a loved one. Rabbis often hear people say, "I haven't been to synagogue for forty years, but now . . . ," and they are sometimes unable to even name what it is they want.

Rabbis, chaplains, physicians, and nurses can testify to the power of prayer to comfort the dying and ease their way. The goal of Jewish prayer by the bedside is not cure—though hope is surely a part of the human genetic map. Jews pray to heal relationships with loved ones and with God. We pray for wholeness—*shleymut*—a word that shares a root with *shalom*, peace.

Rabbis and synagogue *bikkur holim* committees sometimes

bring a brief "healing service" of prayers and psalms to the bedside. Some patients and families find this deeply moving; others see it as a frightening intrusion or a denial of all hope. This is the family's choice.

There are innumerable stories about the impact of praying for and with the dying.

A rabbi sat beside a man who had been in a coma for several days, with a bleak prognosis. The rabbi put his hand on the patient's arm and recited psalms. After a few minutes, the man opened his eyes and regained consciousness. He recovered and went home.

The same rabbi read the same psalms at the bedside of another man in dire condition. That patient died. But his widow was so moved by the rabbi's efforts and attentions that, after years of distance from the Jewish community, she became an active member of a synagogue, where she found much comfort.

A woman sat by the hospital bedside of her husband who was dying of cancer. A member of her synagogue choir, she sang the Shema to him over and over again. While she sang, the electronic monitors showed a gradual slowing of his heart and respiration rates. When she stopped, his breath became labored and his heart raced. She continued her soft, chanting song until her husband achieved a *meta yaffa*—a pleasant death.

END-OF-LIFE DECISIONS: History has taught the Jewish people to be survivors, to defy death sentences, to persevere. The Torah says "Choose life," and the religious principle of preserving human life (*p'kuach nefesh*) is considered a primary mandate. One may break nearly every Jewish law—eat pork, work on the Sabbath—if it might save a life or promote the healing of someone who is ill.

In keeping with this history and tradition, Judaism has always opposed active euthanasia. "Whoever closes the eyes of a *gosses* is considered as if he has taken a life."[4] Some take this to mean that death must be resisted at all costs and by all means. But that is not the only responsible Jewish choice; the tradition views death as part of life and teaches that there is a "time to die." Letting go, accepting the inevitable, and even permitting death to occur are consistent with Jewish law and teaching, too.

The Talmud tells the deathbed story of Rabbi Judah, whose disciples gathered and prayed for his life. The rabbi's maidservant, seeing how the prayers kept the suffering man alive, threw a jar from the roof. The noise distracted the students' prayers long enough to enable the rabbi's soul to depart in peace. The Talmud portrays the woman as a heroine and praises her act of compassion.[5]

While it is forbidden to "hasten death," Jewish authorities throughout the centuries have agreed that it is permissible to remove "impediments" that prolong dying. Of course, the line between "hastening death" and "removing impediments" is not always clear-cut. Rabbi Moses ben Israel Isserles tried to make the distinction in the sixteenth century: "If there is anything that causes a hindrance to the departure of the soul, for example if there is, close to the house, a knocking sound from a wood cutter, or if there is salt on his tongue, and these hinder the departure of the soul, it is permitted to remove them."[6]

The fundamental questions have not changed. Today we ask: When is a respirator (the wood chopper) an impediment to death? Does the removal of a feeding tube or intravenous hydration (salt beneath the tongue or the prayers of the students) "hasten a death?"

Nor is "quality of life" a new concept. In the words of Ben

Sira, a rabbi of the second century B.C.E., "Death is better than a life of pain, and eternal rest than constant sickness."[7]

But even with a medical proxy and living will in hand, end-of-life decisions can be agonizing. Just as every life is unique, the circumstances surrounding the end of each life are unique. Choices about "removing impediments" are best made in consultation with other family members, nurses and doctors, hospice staff, and your rabbi.[8]

FINAL CONFESSION: Many people are surprised to learn that there is a Jewish deathbed confessional prayer called the Viddui. During the Yom Kippur Viddui, the whole congregation rises and symbolically beats its chest while confessing to an alphabetical series of sins. The Viddui recited at the end of life is very different; personal rather than communal, it acknowledges the imperfections of the dying person and seeks a final reconciliation with God.

Unlike the better-known Catholic ritual,[9] reciting the Viddui has nothing to do with insuring the soul's place in the "world-to-come," nor does it, in any way, tempt fate. In the words of the *Shulchan Aruch,*

> If you feel death approaching, recite the Viddui. Be reassured by those around you. Many have said the Viddui and not died, and many have not said the Viddui and have died. If you are unable to recite it aloud, say it in your heart. And if you are unable to recite it, others may recite it with you or for you.[10]

The prayer is recited when death seems imminent; it may be said by the *gosses,* by family members, or by a rabbi. It can be read in Hebrew or English or in both languages. A formal Viddui (samples follow) can be read in sections, with pauses to let people speak from their hearts, to voice regrets or guilt, to ask forgiveness of one another, and to say "I love you."

The Viddui can also be seen as a model for a less formal farewell. People at the bedside can sing a wordless melody—a *niggun*—say a few personal words of good-bye, and recite the Shema together: this, too, is a Viddui.

However, as in all matters concerning the dying, the *gosses* is the one to decide on whether she wants to say or hear this prayer. The Viddui should never be imposed.

The central element of the Viddui is the Shema, the most familiar of all Jewish prayers and the quintessential statement of faith in God's unity. The Shema is the last thing a Jew is supposed to say before death—which is also why it is recited before going to sleep at night. (In case "I should die before I wake.")

The Shema is not a petitionary prayer, nor does it praise God. It is a not really a prayer at all, but the proclamation of God's oneness. It is also an affirmation of Jewish identity and connection.

The Shema ends with the word *Echad,* which means "One." Uttered with "a dying breath," it suggests the ultimate reconciliation of the soul with the Holy One of Blessing, Echad, whom Jews also call Adonai. In many ways, the Shema says "Yes." In its own way, the Shema says "Amen."

CONFESSION
BY THE GRAVELY ILL*

My God and God of all who have gone before me, Author of
life and death,
I turn to You in trust.
Although I pray for life and health, I know that I am mortal.

If this life must soon end, let me die, I pray, at peace.
If only my hands were clean and my heart pure.
I confess that I committed many wrongs and left so much
undone,
Yet I know also the good that I did and tried to do.
May those acts give meaning to my life, and may my errors be
forgiven.
Protector of the bereaved and the helpless, watch over my loved
ones, in whose souls my soul is bound.
You are my Rock and my Redeemer, the Source of mercy and
truth.
Into Your hands I commend my spirit.

Shema Yisrael Adonai Elohenu Adonai Echad.
Hear O Israel, Adonai is our God. Adonai is One.
Adonai is our God. Adonai is our God.[11]

 * *This prayer, like the ones that follow, may be recited on behalf of
 another, i.e.: "Into Your hands we commend his/her spirit."*

VIDDUI:
FINAL CONFESSIONAL PRAYER

My God and God of my fathers and mothers
May my prayer come before You.
Do not ignore my plea.
Please, forgive me for all of the sins
That I sinned before You throughout my lifetime.
I am ashamed of deeds that I have committed.
I regret things that I have done.
Now, O God, take my pain and suffering as atonement.
Forgive my mistakes, for against You have I sinned.

May it be Your will, Adonai, my God and God of my ancestors,
That I sin no more.
In Your great mercy, cleanse me of the sins I have committed,
But not through suffering and disease.
Send me a complete healing along with all those who are ill.

I acknowledge before You, Adonai my God and God of my
    ancestors,
That my healing and my death are in Your hands.
May it be Your will to grant me a complete healing.
If it be Your will that I am to die of this illness,
Let my death be atonement for all the wrongs that I have done
    in my life.
Shelter me in the shadow of Your wings.
Grant me a place in the world to come.

Parent of orphans and Guardian of widows,
Protect my dear ones,
With whose souls my soul is bound.

Into your hand I place my soul.
You have redeemed me, O God of truth.

Shema Yisrael Adonai Elohenu Adonai Echad.
Hear O Israel, The Lord our God, The Lord is One.

Adonai Hu Ha'elohim. Adonai Hu Ha'elohim.
Adonai is God. Adonai is God.

TRANSLATION BY RABBI AMY EILBERG[12]

VIDDUI,
THE FINAL CONFESSION

I acknowledge before the Source of all
That life and death are not in my hands.
Just as I did not choose to be born,
so I do not choose to die.
May it come to pass that I may be healed
but if death is my fate,
then I accept it with dignity
and the loving calm
of one who knows the way of all things.

May my death be honorable,
and may my life be a healing memory
for those who know me.

May my loved ones think well of me
and may my memory bring them joy.

From all those I may have hurt,
I ask forgiveness.
Upon all who have hurt me,
I bestow forgiveness.

As a wave returns to the ocean,
so I return to the Source from which I came.

Shema Yisrael Adonai Elohenu Adonai Echad.
Hear, O Israel,
that which we call God is Oneness itself.
Blessed is the Way of God,
the Way of Life and Death,
of coming and going,
of meeting and loving,
now and forever.
As I was blessed with the one,
so now am I blessed with the other.
Shalom. Shalom. Shalom.

RABBI RAMI M. SHAPIRO[13]

KAYLA'S PRAYER

Listen to my voice,
O Lord our God and God of my ancestors.

I lie here on the brink of life,
Seeking peace, seeking comfort, seeking You.
To You, O Lord, I call and to You, O Lord, I make my
supplication.
Do not ignore my plea.
Let Your mercy flow over me like the waters,
Let the record of my life be a bond between us,
Listen to my voice when I call,
Be gracious to me and answer me.

I have tried, O Lord, to help You complete creation,
I have carried Your Yoke my whole life.
I have tried to do my best.
Count my effort for the good of my soul,
Forgive me for when I have stumbled on Your path.
I can do no more, let my family carry on after me,
Let others carry on after me.

Protector of the helpless, healer of the brokenhearted,
Protect my beloved family with whose souls my own soul is
bound.
Their hearts depended upon mine,
Heal their hearts when they come to depend on You.

Let my soul rest forever under the wings of Your presence,
Grant me a share in the world-to-come.

I have tried to love You with all my heart and with all my soul,
And even though You come to take my soul,
Even though I don't know why You come,
Even though I am angry at the way You take me,
For Your sake I will still proclaim:
Hear, O Israel, the Lord is our God, the Lord alone.
The Lord is with me, I shall not fear.

RABBI LAWRENCE TROSTER[14]

THE MOMENT OF DEATH: The boundary between life and death is an awesome place. From one minute to the next, the spirit or soul is gone. Where there was once energy and consciousness, only a body remains. The room feels entirely different. What is to be done?

Some people simply ask forgiveness of the deceased and sit in silence.

There are many ancient customs surrounding the moment of death, some dating back to biblical times. The eyes are closed and the limbs straightened, the body is laid on the floor, feet facing the door. Some open a window, light a candle, cover the mirrors, and empty any standing water in the room.

Many of these traditions began as folkways, intended to help the soul depart and protect it against evil spirits. Over the centuries, customs rooted in superstition became metaphors for letting go. The open window brings in fresh air. The candle recalls the light that was extinguished by death. Pouring water symbolizes the tears to follow.

The traditional blessing uttered upon witnessing or hearing of a death is:

בָּרוּךְ אַתָּה יְיָ ,אֱלֹהֵינוּ מֶלֶךְ הָעוֹלָם, דַּיַּן הָאֱמֶת.

Baruch ata Adonai Eloheynu melech ha-olam, dayan ha-emet

Holy One of Blessing, Your Presence fills creation, You are indeed the Judge

This statement of total acceptance is a verbal bowing of the head in acknowledgment of what has happened. Like Kaddish, it praises God at a time when God may seem remote, if not cruel.

Many liberal rabbis do not recite the *Dayan ha-Emet* blessing to mourners, especially in untimely circumstances. How can the death of a child be the result of God's judgment? Is the accidental death of a husband and father in the prime of his life a "ruling" against him?

But for most people, words are nearly meaningless at the moment of death. Consolation comes later.

As soon as someone is able, there are a few official telephone calls to make. If the death occurs at home or anywhere other than a medical facility, notify the doctor and police (911). Contact the funeral home, and inform your rabbi and/or your loved one's rabbi.

UNEXPECTED DEATHS: Although accompanying a loved one through a final illness is difficult and painful, it does give family and friends time to prepare themselves for the end. When you know that death is imminent, the move into mourning is more like shifting weight from one foot to the other, but sudden death lifts you up by the back of the neck and drops you, shattered, into the valley of the shadow.

People who lose a loved one by violence, accident, or sudden illness are doubly bereaved. A fatal heart attack, a stillbirth, a car crash, means there was no time to make peace or say good-bye or promise to remember. When a child or young person dies, it feels like life itself has been violated.

The Jewish path through mourning does not try to make sense of such losses, nor does it attempt to make the pain go away. It is only a lifeline, a way to get through.

....

CHAPTER FOUR

HONORING
THE DEAD

IN THE AFTERMATH OF A DEATH, MOURNERS ENTER A kind of no-man's-land of grief. Jewish tradition provides the bereaved with a name for this place—*aninut*. Those who inhabit this dark and raw state of mourning are called *onenim*, whose only responsibility is *kevod ha-met*, showing honor to the dead.

ANINUT: THE HOLLOW DAYS

Aninut lasts from the moment of death until the end of the funeral. As with all aspects of mourning, people experience the initial shock of death in different ways. There may be silence and numbness, or uncontrollable sobbing. After a long illness, mourners may feel relief. After an accident or other catastrophic loss, disbelief and rage. There is no need to stifle any feeling during *aninut*. In the words of Ben Sira, "Bewail the dead. Hide not your grief. Do not restrain your mourning."

Jewish law constructs an especially strong protective "fence" around *onenim,* who are exempt from all regular activity. They conduct no business, eat no meat, drink no wine, attend no social gatherings, and refrain from sexual relations. They are not even counted in a *minyan* or even required to say the blessing over bread.

In order to protect the bereaved from well-meaning but premature attempts at condolence, friends do not visit before the funeral. The Talmud advises, "Do not try to comfort your friend while the body of his deceased lies before him."[1]

Aninut builds a moat around mourners, not only so that they can weep but also so they can concentrate on making final arrangements for the dead, such as selecting a coffin and meeting with the rabbi to discuss the eulogy. This responsibility does not contradict the injunction to "bewail the dead"; indeed, it is complementary since both tasks insist that the mourner face the reality of what has happened. There is no turning away from death during *aninut.*

There is no reason for mourners to do everything, however. The mundane but necessary arrangements—from selecting pallbearers to placing a newspaper obituary—can be overwhelming. Funeral directors will do much of this work. And whenever possible, the bereaved should be relieved of daily responsibilities such as cooking, answering the phone, or driving children to school. Spouses, siblings, adult children and/or close friends can and should assist.

For *onenim* who have the energy and inclination, this is a good time to write down what they are feeling. Some people begin a bereavement journal during *aninut,* others compose their thoughts in the form of a letter to the deceased. These words may even become the basis for a eulogy.

KEVOD HA-MET: CARING FOR THE DEAD

Judaism views the human body as one of the miracles of creation, a reverence that continues even after death. The corpse, in Hebrew, *met*, is treated with the exquisite respect owed to a vessel that held a human spirit. Every effort is made to recall the personness of the body and to avoid treating it merely as an object.

This is a difficult and consuming task, which is part of the reason Jewish law requires burial as quickly as possible. Until the funeral is over, the care of the dead is the sole focus of the bereaved and their community. Tradition mandates speed in burying the body so that attention can shift to the care of the living and the work of grief.

The *mitzvah* of *kevod ha-met*, honoring the dead, is not abstract or sentimental. Jewish law is explicit about the details of caring for the body. Jews who grow up without any exposure to these customs are often amazed by and grateful for their wisdom. It is never easy to make choices about the disposition of a loved one's body. But the parameters provided by Jewish tradition can ease the disorientation and loneliness by connecting the decisions about how, where, and when to generations past and generations to follow.

CHOOSING HOW TO HONOR THE DEAD: The very first phone call to the funeral home is an act of *kevod ha-met*. Due to Judaism's requirement for timely burial, the funeral director must collect some basic information immediately: for example, the deceased's full name and Hebrew name, parents' names and their Hebrew names, place of birth, Social Security number, veteran's information, and cause of death.

The funeral director (or "counselor") will set up an appointment within twenty-four hours to gather other information (such as the deed to a funeral plot) and begin making final arrangements. This meeting usually includes the primary mourners (a surviving spouse and/or adult children), though another supportive family member or close friend may also attend.

Unless advance plans have been made, survivors will be asked to make decisions about the preparation of the body for burial and funeral arrangements (The service will be planned with the officiating rabbi or cantor.) A casket must be selected, limousines ordered, and an obituary written and sent. There will be many other questions as well:

Do you wish *taharah*? Shrouds or clothing? Would you like to hire a *shomer*? Is there a family rabbi who will officiate or should the funeral director put you in touch with local clergy? Will flowers be permitted? Do you have a list of pallbearers? Will you be sitting *shiva*?

Although this list may sound overwhelming, the following pages explain the meaning of these words and the implications of the choices. The funeral director will take care of the details, according to your specifications.

TIMING: Traditionally, burial occurs within a day, a custom based on a line in the Torah: "You shall bury him the same day. . . . His body should not remain all night."[2]

There have always been exceptions to this rule. Burials never take place on the Sabbath or during holidays. Delays are sanctioned when the body has to be transported for burial, if close relatives need time to travel to the funeral, for a legally or medically mandated autopsy, and to accommodate the rabbi's schedule.

Even so, the goal is to expedite burial in order to preserve the dignity of the deceased. The body is described as *nireh v'eyno ro'eh,* one who can be seen but who cannot see—a status that cries out for resolution. In this state, bodies are to be handled as little as possible, except for the simple rituals of religious purification called *taharah.*

In the past, speedy burial kept the body—which was laid out in the family home—from starting to decompose in the presence of loved ones. But even today, when bodies are removed from sight and refrigerated to prevent decay, there is still the danger of objectifying the body, of thinking about the *met* as an "it" rather than "he" or "she."

The other reason for burying the body as soon as possible is to shorten the amount of time mourners spend in *aninut.* Only after the funeral does the focus shift from *kevod ha-met,* honoring the dead, to *nichum avelim,* comforting the bereaved. The insistence on a timely burial is not a denial of death but a reflection of Judaism's unfailing emphasis on the needs of the living.

GUARDIANS OF RESPECT: Jewish tradition requires that a body be accompanied at all times. In ancient times, guardians (*shomrim*) protected the body from scavengers and thieves, but for many centuries they have guarded against disrespect and indifference. The *mitzvah* called *shemira* (guarding) is a singular way to honor the deceased.

Friends or synagogue members usually act as *shomrim,* accompanying the body from home or hospital to the mortuary and then taking turns until the funeral. *Shomrim* stay near the body and read psalms, especially Psalm 23, "The Lord is my Shepherd," and Psalm 91, which speaks of God as a consoler, protector, and redeemer. Jewish funeral homes offer the services of paid *shomrim* to read psalms near the body, and later, beside the casket.

Among liberal Jews, this custom has largely fallen by the wayside. Since funeral homes are staffed twenty-four hours a day, the body is technically never left alone. Given the fact that bodies are refrigerated until burial, *shomrim* rarely sit right beside the body. Even so, some synagogue *hevra kadishas,* or bereavement committees, offer *shemira* if the family wishes it.

TAHARAH: The physical preparation of the body for burial is called *taharah,* a word that means "purification." The rituals of *taharah*—which include ceremonial washing, dressing in shrouds, and placing the body into the coffin—are considered one of the greatest *mitzvot* a Jew can perform. It is a *hesed shel emet,* an eternal act of kindness, one that cannot be repaid.

Taharah is the ultimate expression of respect for the physical person. It is a communal acknowledgment that every individual is made in the image of God and is therefore, in some ineffable way, *kadosh,* or holy. *Taharah* is also a daunting *mitzvah* because it entails handling a dead body, something that most people avoid. Those who have done it, however, report that *taharah* is one of the most awe-inspiring experiences of their lives.[3]

Taharah is done by staff at some Jewish funeral homes, but traditionally it is the work of a voluntary group called a *hevra kadisha,* usually translated as "burial society," although the literal meaning is "holy society." A *hevra kadisha* is an association of unpaid, anonymous Jewish laymen and laywomen who have studied the laws and customs of *taharah* and learned the practical how-tos of the *mitzvah* by watching others with more experience. Women attend to the bodies of women, men to the bodies of men. Family members do not participate because it is considered too painful for them to handle the body of their loved one.

Every Orthodox community is served by a *hevra kadisha* that provides *taharah* to any Jew who requests it, usually regardless of affiliation and free of any charge. *Hevra kadisha* members are never paid. Wherever a fee is attached to *taharah,* it is for the cost of supplies only. Should this minimal cost be prohibitive, it will be waived.

Although several generations of liberal Jews abandoned *taharah* and followed secular customs, the liberal community has begun to reclaim the practice. A few congregations have even established their own burial societies to provide *taharah* to their members or to any Jewish family that requests it for a loved one.[4] (See "Bibliography and Resources.")

The essential religious gesture of *taharah* is a ritual washing. As in many other aspects of life and the life cycle, Jews use water to signal a fundamental change in personal status, and/or to transform what is *tameh,* or ritually impure, into something *tahor,* pure. *Taharah* for the dead echoes the experience of *mikvah* for the living—where immersion in a body of "living water" commemorates a personal transformation.[5]

First, the body is placed on a table with a drain and methodically washed with clean, lukewarm water.[6] Ever mindful of the person's modesty, only the body parts being washed are exposed. The hair is combed, the fingernails cleaned.

Then the body is raised up to a standing position and held in the arms of members of the *hevra kadisha* while others pour a steady stream of water—twenty-four quarts—over it. After this, the members of the *hevra* say three times: "*Tahor hoo*" (He is pure.) Or "*Tahor hee*" (She is pure.)

Taharah is performed somberly and quietly, usually beginning with a prayer, the *Hamol,* which asks God to forgive the deceased. When the *hevra kadisha* is finished with their task, every member addresses the body to ask its forgiveness for any inadvertent disrespect. Other prayers may be recited, too.

The rituals and prayers of the *hevra kadisha* vary from city to city, and even from one burial society to the next. Since it is the nature of liberal Judaism to seek meaningful ways to give new expression to ancient practices, liberal burial societies sometimes depart from certain customs. Thus, for example, family members who wish to participate tend to be welcomed. Or the body will be sung to, as a final farewell.

Blessing recited before *taharah:*

Source of kindness and compassion, whose ways are ways of mercy and truth, You have commanded us to act with loving kindness and righteousness towards the dead, and to engage in their proper burial. Grant us the courage and strength to properly perform this work, this holy task of cleaning and washing the body, dressing the dead in shrouds, and burying the deceased. Guide our hands and hearts as we do this work and enable us to fulfill this commandment of love. Help us to see Your face in the face of the deceased, even as we see You in the faces of those who share this task with us. Source of life and death, be with us now and always.[7]

SHROUDS: The traditional clothing for burying the dead are *tachrichim,* simple white shrouds. Their use dates back to Rabbi Simeon ben Gamliel II, who, in the second century of the Common Era, asked to be buried in inexpensive linen garments. The custom—which set both a decorous minimum and a limit on ostentation—has been followed by observant Jews ever since:[8] "Whoever heaps elaborate shrouds upon the dead transgresses the injunction against wanton destruction. Such a one disgraces the deceased."[9]

The universal use of shrouds protected the poor from embarrassment at not being able to afford lavish burial clothes. Since shrouds have no pockets, wealth or status cannot be expressed or acknowledged in death. In every generation, these garments reaffirmed a fundamental belief in human equality.

Shrouds are white and entirely hand-stitched. They are made without buttons, zippers, or fasteners. *Tachrichim* come in muslin or linen, fabrics that recall the garments of the ancient Hebrew priesthood. There is little difference in appearance or cost between them; the funeral home may or may not offer a choice.

Tachrichim come packaged in sets for men and women. Regardless of gender, they include shirt, pants, a head covering, and a belt. Men may also be wrapped in a *kittel*, a simple, white ceremonial jacket that some Jews wear on Yom Kippur, at the Passover seder, and under the wedding canopy.

If the body has been prepared for burial with *taharah,* the body will automatically be dressed in *tachrichim.* Jewish funeral homes and *hevra kadishas* have a supply on hand, and the cost may be covered by their honorarium. If you are in an area where there is no Jewish funeral home or burial society, the local mortuary may permit you to prepare the body according to Jewish law. A Jewish funeral home in the nearest city can send a set of shrouds by overnight mail.

In addition to *tachrichim,* some Jews are wrapped in the prayer shawl, or *tallit,* in which they prayed. Every *tallit* is tied with four sets of knotted fringes (*tzitzit*), which symbolize the *mitzvot*, the commandments incumbent upon Jews. Before the *tallit* is placed on a body for burial, however, one of the sets of fringes is cut to demonstrate that the person is no longer bound by the religious obligations of the living.

When only men wore *tallitot*, only men were buried in them. But any woman who wore a prayer shawl in life—an increasingly common custom—is generally accorded the same treatment. This may be an issue if the *hevra kadisha* is comprised of Orthodox Jews who object to women's use of *tallitot;* mourners should be clear about their wishes.

Tachrichim swaddle the entire body, including the face, so that the deceased is both clothed and protected against the gaze of other people. If shrouds are used, the body is placed in the casket, which is then closed.

A small bag of earth from Israel may be placed in the coffin—another reminder of the biblical phrase, "For you are dust, and to dust shall you return"[10] and a sign of the importance of the land of Israel to Jews throughout the centuries. (Jewish funeral homes generally offer this option.) Notes or other personal mementos are sometimes placed in the casket as well.

Some people express a wish to be buried in a particular dress or suit and some mourners are uncomfortable with the idea of shrouds for a family member who abhorred all religious tradition and trappings. Liberal Jews sometimes honor the tradition of simplicity by requesting a minimum of handling, no cosmetics on the body, and a closed casket.

AUTOPSY AND ORGAN DONATION: Many people are familiar with the traditional Jewish prohibition against autopsies, which were seen as a desecration of the body. However, there have always been exceptions to this law, as when civil authorities require medical examination of the body in cases of homicide, suicide, and some accidental deaths. Autopsies are also permitted when they might provide medical knowledge that can help others.

Indeed, the religious precept of *p'kuach nefesh* (the saving of a life), is one of Judaism's paramount values. All liberal rabbinic authorities and most Orthodox rabbis support organ donation as a holy act and the antithesis of desecration. "There can be no greater *kevod ha-met* [respect for the dead] than to bring healing to the living," writes Rabbi Isaac Klein, a Conservative movement authority on Jewish law and a supporter of organ donation.[11]

This *matan chaim*, or gift of life, is the simplest and most important of all medical directives. (See "Bibliography and Resources" for information about how to obtain an organ donation card.)

EMBALMING, VIEWING THE BODY, AND WAKES: Embalming is the process of preventing decay by treating the body with preservatives. Fluids are injected into the veins and, in some cases, organs are removed to delay decomposition and promote a "lifelike" appearance. Since refrigeration has mostly done away with the public health rationale for embalming, the only reason to do it now is cosmetic.

Judaism prohibits embalming, artificial arranging of limbs, and any use of cosmetics on a corpse on the grounds that these practices violate the dignity of the corpse, *nivul ha-met*, which is the opposite of *kevod ha-met*. The goal of embalming—to prevent its decomposition—runs counter to the mandate that the body be returned to the earth as naturally as possible.

> You return to the soil
> for from it you were taken
> For you are dust, and to dust shall you return.[12]

Exceptions are made if the funeral must be postponed for a lengthy period, if the body must be transported overseas, or if the civil government requires it. In the United States, embalming is not a legal requirement.

Wakes, open caskets, and viewing the body are Christian burial customs, familiar to most Jews through books and popular culture if not firsthand experience. From a Jewish perspective, however, these practices run counter to the principle of *kevod hamet* by turning the body into a thing that is manipulated for the benefit of others. In a tradition where memory is considered a primary obligation and blessing, most people prefer to remember the deceased as a vibrant human being rather than as a dressed-up corpse.

In some instances, however, family members who were far away at the time of death insist on seeing the body one last time before burial, as a way of saying good-bye or even to convince themselves of the reality of the death. This kind of viewing can be private, and often takes place just prior to the funeral. (Since some use of cosmetics is usually necessary, this precludes *taharah* and traditional shrouds.)

Wakes, memorial events where mourners receive guests prior to the funeral—sometimes with the body on view—are antithetical to Jewish tradition. Condolences from friends, colleagues, and neighbors are offered and accepted after the funeral, when *shiva* begins.

CASKETS: Abraham and Sarah, the first Jews, were buried without coffins. That is still the practice in the land of Israel, where shrouded bodies are laid to rest directly in the earth that Jews have always considered holy.

However, three generations later, when Joseph, the son of Jacob and Rachel, died, he was embalmed and buried in a coffin, as was the practice in Egypt, where he lived. Ever since Joseph, Jews have tended to follow at least some of the burial traditions of the cultures in which they found themselves. Thus, by the 1600s, coffins were customary among the Jews of Europe.[13]

The Hebrew word for "coffin" is *aron,* which means "ark," a word more commonly associated with another container that holds another sacred object: the *aron kodesh,* or holy ark, where Torah scrolls are kept in the synagogue. From medieval times to our own, Jewish *aronot* have tended to be simple. A traditional casket is a plain wooden box. No satin lining inside. No handles outside. Although metal nails are permitted, wooden pegs are preferred. Since the goal of a Jewish coffin is to permit the body to return to the earth as naturally as possible, holes are drilled in the bottom.

This type of coffin, which is considered "kosher" or ritually fit, looks rough, even crude, beside others on display in the casket room of a funeral home. Coffins come in a wide range of finishes, materials, and prices. Polished mahogany caskets with elaborate silver hardware and plush, satin linings, may cost several thousand dollars. By contrast, a plain "kosher casket" may sell for a few hundred dollars.

Selecting a casket is always a strange experience. However, mourners who must purchase a coffin in the immediate aftermath of a loved one's death and wish to honor the tradition of simplicity have no real need of setting foot inside a casket display room. Simply tell the funeral director that you want the "least expensive kosher casket available." In this context, "kosher" means "in conformance with Jewish law." He or she will know what you mean.

Even so, stark simplicity is not an easy choice. The temptation to spend money on burial and mourning is probably as old as humanity. A beautiful casket seems to prove a family's devotion and the importance of the deceased. The rabbis who codified the Babylonian Talmud (circa 500 C.E.) were familiar with this issue:

People used to bring food to a house of mourning: the wealthy brought it in baskets of silver and gold, the poor in baskets of willow twigs. And the poor felt ashamed. Therefore our sages taught that everyone should use baskets of willow twigs.

People used to serve drinks in a house of mourning: the wealthy served them in white glasses, the poor served them in less expensive colored glasses. And the poor felt ashamed. Therefore our sages taught that everyone should serve drinks in colored glasses.

People used to bring out the deceased for burial: the rich on a tall state bed, ornamented and covered with rich coverlets, the poor on a plain bier. And the poor felt ashamed. Therefore a law was established that all should be brought out on a plain bier.[14]

These rulings enforced a kind of democracy in death, acknowledging the elemental equality of all human beings. In the words of the Midrash, "A baby enters the world with closed hands. A person leaves the world with open hands. The first says, 'The world is mine.' The second says, 'I can take nothing with me.' "[15]

For centuries, Jewish families have taken the money that might have been spent on a fancy casket and given it to a charity that had meaning to the deceased. A memorial that benefits the living is considered a far more meaningful show of respect and love than an expensive coffin. (See Chapter 9, The Consolations of Memory.)

BURIAL PLOTS AND CEMETERIES: A Jewish burial site is called a *bet ha-olam*—an eternal home, the permanent address of memory. Traditionally, Jews are buried with family members, a tradition that dates back to the book of Genesis, where Abraham purchases a cave as the grave site for Sarah, his wife. Several chapters later, Abraham's grandson, Joseph, asks that his remains be transported from Egypt to the family plot in the land of his father, Jacob.

Throughout history, purchasing land for a Jewish cemetery has been a primary concern, and one of the community's first responsibilities whenever Jews moved to a new place. Adult Jews were expected to purchase a grave site for themselves and their families in a cemetery run by and for Jews.

Many people still follow this custom, knowing that they are sparing family members future anguish and expense. However, the modern aversion to talking about or planning for death includes much of the Jewish community, too, so that Jewish mourners often find themselves in the unfortunate position of having to select and purchase a plot in the wake of a loved one's death.

In communities with a sizable or historic Jewish presence, there are separate Jewish cemeteries or a designated Jewish section in a larger cemetery that is set off by a fence or hedge and has its own entrance.

Jewish cemeteries in America run the gamut from old, crowded burial grounds with headstones in all shapes and sizes, to "memorial parks" where only flat, uniform markers are permitted. Cemeteries are owned and operated as businesses, separate from funeral homes. The sale of a plot is a real estate transaction like any other. Upon payment to the cemetery (or its broker), the owner receives title to the property, which can be sold or inherited like any other piece of land. (In Jewish cemeteries, resale will be legally limited to other Jews.) Plots vary in price from one part of the country to the next, and from one cemetery to the next.

If the deceased did not own a plot, a funeral director will assist the family in locating one, though the cost will be separate from the mortuary charges. Driving around in cemeteries "shopping" for a plot on the day after a loved one dies is a terribly distressing task; good reason—difficult as it is—to discuss the subject before it becomes urgent.

Purchasing a funeral plot has probably never been more complicated than it is today. Given the geographical realities of modern life—with families scattered all over the country—it is not easy to decide where to buy a plot: Near the homestead where a surviving parent resides? Back "home" or near the retirement community? Close to a grown child? The prevalence of divorce and remarriage complicates this decision, too, unless the deceased made his or her wishes known.

The question of where to bury non-Jewish family members

is often a source of conflict and pain. Traditionally, Jews are buried in cemeteries that have been consecrated for Jews only. (Judaism's insistence on the importance of a dedicated, communal burial space is not unique; many cultures and religions also set themselves apart in death.) The charters or bylaws of most Jewish cemeteries explicitly forbid burial of non-Jews within their precincts.

There are a variety of accommodations to this problem. Some cemeteries owned by Reform synagogues permit the burial of non-Jewish spouses. Some Jewish cemeteries designate a special section for intermarried couples. Others will bury non-Jewish spouses adjacent to their Jewish families, just outside the legal boundaries of the Jewish section. Some families avoid the issue by purchasing plots in a nonsectarian cemetery.

MAUSOLEUMS: The Jewish custom of returning the body to the earth is rooted in the Torah. The image of returning to the dust is so ancient and ingrained, the idea of placing human remains in an aboveground vault strikes many as sacrilegious or just plain un-Jewish. Aboveground burial is fairly uncommon throughout the Jewish world and many rabbis will not officiate at an interment in a mausoleum.

Jewish law and custom also weigh heavily against the use of in-ground vaults when their only purpose is to preserve the body. However, in-ground vaults are accepted if the ground is unstable or waterlogged and local authorities require the use of a permanent lining around the coffin to keep the earth from shifting or sinking.

A columbarium is a vault with niches for urns containing the ashes of the dead. Given Judaism's traditional aversion to crema-

tion, very few rabbis are comfortable attending, much less officiating, at an "insertion" in such a facility.

CREMATION: The *halachic* prohibition against cremation is
absolute. The Jewish distaste for cremation is based on respect
for the body and for the natural process of "dust to dust." Burial
returns the body to its source, reuniting one part of creation with
the rest of it; by contrast, burning the body seems a desecration
of something created in God's image, and even a form of violence. Of course, in modern times the Holocaust has turned the
very word into a hideous reminder of ovens, chimneys, and the
charred remains of millions of Jews who were denied their
humanity in death as in life.

Despite the legal, historical, and emotional arguments against
it, many Jews express wishes and even make arrangements for
their own cremation. This may be done with the intention of
sparing the family the expense and supposed trauma of a funeral.
Jewish funeral homes will arrange for cremation at a non-Jewish
facility, and sell boxes and urns for storing ashes.

Among liberal Jews, cremation does not preclude sitting
shiva, saying Kaddish, or observing other traditions of mourning. All liberal rabbis will offer comfort and counsel to bereaved
families regardless of the disposition of the body. Some Jewish
clergy (cantors as well as rabbis) will conduct a service at the
funeral home when cremation is planned; however, others feel
they cannot. Some rabbis will lead a memorial service in the synagogue, or a *shiva minyan* in the family's home at some time following a cremation.

A loved one's wish to be cremated can create dilemmas and
conflicts for his survivors. Family members who would prefer to

follow a more traditional Jewish path may be asked to choose between obeying Dad's last wishes and violating their own beliefs or needs. And since most families include differing religious interpretations and levels of observance, cremation can lead to arguments and bad feelings. There is no simple solution to the debate between honoring the deceased's wishes (*kevod ha-met*) and the equally legitimate need to comfort the mourner (*nichum avelim*). A thoughtful rabbi may be able to serve as a helpful sounding board in such cases.

CHAPTER FIVE

·······························

THE FUNERAL

THE HEBREW FOR FUNERAL IS *LEVAYAH*, A WORD THAT means "accompanying." Although a rabbi's or cantor's presence at a funeral is important, there is no religious requirement that clergy be present. Family and community are responsible for burying their own dead, since only people who knew the deceased in life can show them the honor they deserve in death.

Levayah is incumbent upon the immediate family, but the *mitzvah* extends to the entire community. The notion of a "private funeral," with only immediate family in attendance, runs counter to Jewish sensibilities not only because it deprives mourners of human contact and comfort, but also because it deprives friends, colleagues, neighbors, and acquaintances of the opportunity to grieve, to show respect, and to perform the *mitzvah* of *levayah*.

While Jewish funerals are often inspirational and comforting, their primary purpose is not to make the bereaved feel better. Unlike the custom of other religious traditions, Jewish funerals do not address the ideas of heaven, redemption, and ultimate reunion. The focus is on the life of the deceased and thus on the unique dimensions of their loss.

Traditional Jewish funerals are almost stark in their simplicity. The casket is covered with a simple cloth called a pall and displayed without floral adornment. There is no soothing background music. The casket is lowered into the ground in full view of the family, and then the bereaved take up a shovel to cover the coffin.

The funeral is a confrontation with the finality of death. The open grave looks like a wound in the earth, which is like the wound in the bereaved heart. Once the grave is closed, however, there is absolutely nothing left to be done for the dead. Afterward, there is only mourning.

A MEANINGFUL FUNERAL: Based on past experience, many people think of funerals as empty, dishonest ordeals. The services seemed long and incomprehensible. Even worse, the eulogies echoed with hollow platitudes intoned by a stranger. With those memories as models, it is no wonder that some people opt for private services or cremation without any ceremony at all. But when mourners understand the rituals and embrace the traditions of simplicity and honesty, Jewish funerals can be dignified, beautiful, and healing: a crowning tribute to the deceased and an emotional catharsis for the bereaved.

Funerals are often divided into two parts, service and interment, though they are combined when the funeral service takes place at the graveside. The liturgy is brief; a few traditional psalms and prayers and the eulogy (or eulogies). Funerals tend not to be highly "creative." Bereaved people are usually in too much pain to explore or write alternative services. Nevertheless, the more mourners know about the rituals and customs, the more meaningful and memorable the funeral can be.

WHERE AND WHEN: Until modern times, most funeral services were conducted in the family home, a practice that is now rare. Today, funerals are held in one of four places: the funeral home chapel (probably the most common choice), a synagogue sanctuary or chapel, the cemetery chapel, or beside the grave. Not all of these options are available in all cities or towns; for example, some cemeteries do not have a chapel on their grounds.

The synagogue is the traditional site for Jewish life-cycle events. When a coffin is brought into the sanctuary that was a scene of joyful events in the life of the deceased—weddings and baby namings, bar and bat mitzvah ceremonies—death takes its place in the unending circle of life.

Chapels at mortuaries and cemeteries have several practical advantages: the body is already (or will be transported) there, they are outfitted to accommodate funerals, and they usually have ample parking. In the past, synagogue funerals were reserved for rabbis and scholars only; today, they may be an option for congregation members only, but customs vary from one temple to the next.

A graveside service, which combines the two elements of the funeral, is the preferred choice in some communities. A tent and chairs may be set up beside the grave, but these are usually reserved for family only, leaving others to stand during the service.

Jewish law prohibits funerals from taking place on Shabbat or holidays, which are set aside for celebration and/or religious services. The tradition encourages morning funerals as a demonstration of the family's willingness to fulfill the *mitzvah*. However, many funerals take place at noon or early afternoon, to permit as many people as possible to attend. Timing may also depend upon the rabbi's schedule and availability of a sanctuary or chapel.

GATHERING: Just prior to the funeral, the immediate family meets with the rabbi either in the rabbi's study or in a special room set up for this purpose at the chapel. This is a private time for mourners to assemble and compose themselves, and for the rabbi to review the order of the service. It also prevents the understandable but intrusive custom of guests lining up to offer condolences before the burial rather than afterward.

The meeting with the rabbi before the funeral is also a common time and place for *k'riah*, the ritual rending of garments.

K'RIAH: Rending garments is an elemental, physical enactment of the feeling that death has torn the world apart. The ripping of fabric is the sound of a heart breaking. In the Bible, Jacob tears his clothes when he is told that Joseph, his son, has been killed.[1] *K'riah* usually takes place immediately before the funeral, though sometimes it is done immediately after the funeral, at the grave, or even when someone first hears of the death.

The ritual is very simple. Family members stand as the rabbi explains the meaning of *k'riah*. Some rabbis rip the fabric in silence, others recite a blessing. The traditional *b'racha* for *k'riah* is the *Dayan ha-Emet*, which is the blessing said upon hearing any bad news. It is a statement of total acceptance. Some rabbis will use a different blessing or reading. (See "The Moment of Death" in Chapter 3.)

בָּרוּךְ אַתָּה יְיָ, אֱלֹהֵינוּ מֶלֶךְ הָעוֹלָם, דַּיַּן הָאֱמֶת.

Baruch ata Adonai Elohenu melech ha-olam, dayan ha-emet

Holy One of Blessing, Your Presence fills creation, You
are indeed the Judge.

According to the traditional ritual, men tear the lapel of a
sport coat or jacket; women tear a sweater or blouse. Tearing real
clothing fell out of use in the liberal community several generations ago. Today, mourners usually substitute a symbolic black
ribbon for an item of clothing. The ribbons are provided by the
funeral home and pinned onto the lapel of immediate family
members. (Traditionally, on the left side for parents; on the right
for others.) Some mourners rip a tie or scarf to create a more personal symbol of loss than a ribbon manufactured solely for the
purpose of *k'riah.*

The ribbon (or torn garment) is usually worn only during the
week of *shiva,* except on Shabbat, when it is removed so as to
protect the joyful quality of the Sabbath. However, some liberal
Jews wear the ribbon throughout *shloshim* as a public declaration
of mourning. (See Chapter 8.)

FLOWERS AND MUSIC: As mourners and friends walk into
the chapel for most Jewish funerals, they will see the coffin
already in place, covered by a simple cloth pall.[2] There are no
flowers. The room will be quiet, since no background music can
fill up the silence left by this death.

The rabbis of the Talmud viewed flowers as remnants of
pagan customs and ruled them inappropriate for Jewish funerals.
There is also a sense that money spent on flowers is better spent
on a more meaningful tribute of charity. Newspaper obituaries

often request that no flowers be sent and list charities or organizations for donations instead. (See "*Tzedakah*" in Chapter 9.)

Nevertheless, some families do display flowers, either because they remember floral arrangements from the funerals of their youth or because flowers meant a great deal to the deceased. In Israel, flowers are common at graves—especially the graves of soldiers. This "exception to the rule" is not unprecedented as there are some Talmudic references to ornaments—"spices and twigs"—at burials.[3]

Jewish funeral homes generally accommodate requests for flowers; however, some synagogues forbid floral displays at funerals within their doors. If flowers are important to you, this may be a consideration in deciding where to hold the service.

Music is viewed in much the same way as flowers: as a distraction from grief, and a non-Jewish practice. At a traditional Jewish funeral, the only music is the cantor's chanting of the prayer *El Malei Rachamim*—"God Filled with Compassion." (The text appears below.) The heartbreaking singularity of the song is part of its power.

The addition of music is probably the most striking modern change in the funeral liturgy. Some liberal rabbis and cantors lead the congregation in singing a somber *niggun*, a wordless melody, or Psalm 23, or another Hebrew or Jewish song that held special meaning for the deceased. Sometimes, family members will request that a piece of music that was loved by the departed be played while everyone listens in silence—a kind of musical eulogy. Funeral chapels usually have an organ on the premises and are able to arrange for other instruments, such as a cello.

THE FUNERAL LITURGY: Compared with the specific rules and requirements for the preparation of the body and its burial, there are surprisingly few liturgical requirements for a funeral service. In general, and with many minor variations, a Jewish funeral consists of three parts: opening psalms and readings, the eulogy (*hesped* in Hebrew), and closing prayers, including *El Malei Rachamim*.

Although any Jew may conduct a funeral, nearly all are led by rabbis or cantors. Participation by family and friends is an option, but this is rarely a time for creative liturgies, and families tend to leave the service to the clergy. The officiating rabbi or cantor reads or chants all of the prayers, though in some chapels prayer books are distributed for congregational or responsive reading.

There is no real "processional" at a Jewish funeral, as the casket is already in the room prior to its beginning. One common custom is for the family to enter through a side door just before the service begins, after others have been seated.

OPENING PRAYERS: The funeral begins with psalms, prayers, and poems. The rabbi or cantor will select pieces he or she feels best suited to the deceased and to the family's wishes, and mourners can request specific readings.

At some point in the service—or later at graveside—the rabbi will read Psalm 23. The comforting words "The Lord is my Shepherd" take on new meaning every time they are spoken at a funeral. The valley of the shadow of death is no metaphor for the bereaved; it is a place they know all too well.

EULOGY: The *hesped* is the heart of the funeral service. Its main purpose is to praise the deceased for the unique good he or she represented and did in the world. In the words of the *Shulchan Aruch*, the purpose of the *hesped* is to "Lament the dead in words that break the heart."[4]

The best eulogies are not necessarily great orations, nor are they lists of accomplishments, achievements, and honors, however impressive they may be. Great eulogies are made of real stories that evoke genuine emotion. They are full of anecdotes. They employ phrases and jokes that the departed used to favor. They recall a life that changed the world forever by having been part of it.

The best eulogies are honest. Jewish tradition actually prohibits exaggeration and invention. To call someone "saintly" who was no such thing makes a mockery of the good that the person actually did. Nevertheless, the idea that everyone deserves a *hesped* reflects the belief that every human being is of value. It is up to the living to discern the nature of that value, whether it was professional brilliance, personal integrity, a love of beauty, devotion to the Jewish people, love of family, or simple kindness.

WHO DELIVERS THE EULOGY: The most moving tributes come from people who knew the deceased well, which argues for having a family member deliver the eulogy. However, since many mourners are unable to speak in public at this time, the rabbi who officiates at the funeral usually writes and delivers it—but always as the family's representative. Even rabbis who did not know the deceased can write wonderful eulogies if they are provided with enough information.

During the meeting to plan the funeral with the family, the focus is on the eulogy. The rabbi or cantor will try to get a sense of the departed, to insure that nothing important is omitted, and to collect vivid stories. It's a good idea to assemble a few people who knew the departed well for this meeting. One person's memories and stories—regardless of how close they were—will inevitably yield a one-sided picture. If possible, have members of different generations present: spouse, children, siblings, grand-children. This may be a good way to involve young people, who often feel that their grief is ignored.

The rabbi will ask about your loved one's personality, charac-teristics, and gifts that were unique and precious to you. What mattered most to him? How did your loved one relate to her family? Was he known by a nickname? Were there certain words or phrases everyone associated with him? Was she an avid reader? A hobbyist? What music did she love? What made her laugh? Eulogies that summon laughter are healing and entirely appropriate because they recall the whole person, not just his or her death.

The rabbi will also need to know the deceased's Hebrew name, which is included in the *El Malei Rachamim* prayer. Hebrew names usually include parents' names as well: *Shimon ben Avraham v'Leah,* Simon son of Abraham and Leah.

To prepare for the meeting with the rabbi or cantor, put out a photograph album or some favorite snapshots. Pictures can help prompt stories and unbidden memories, and it is a good way to make your loved one come alive to a rabbi who may not have known him or her.

Don't hesitate to speak honestly. The rabbi should know if, for example, the deceased was a religious skeptic, or whether there was a long-standing family estrangement. Although you don't have to go into great detail, it's important to mention such things to help avoid jarring misstatements.

Again, the rabbi or cantor need not be the one—or the only one—to deliver a eulogy. If mourners decide to speak, it's impor-tant to set time limits. Good eulogies do not ramble, and too many reminiscences can become painful. The rabbi can help to set limits, determine how many people should speak, or come up with alternatives: if several people want to speak, for instance, they can share their memories during *shiva* services instead. (See Chapter 7.)

Mourners should never feel pressure to speak at a loved one's funeral. For many people, the pain is too great to try to give public voice to their feelings. Even if you are accustomed to public speaking, even if you are a rabbi who has delivered hundreds of eulogies, at a loved one's funeral, all you need to be is the *onen*, the bereaved.

All funerals are sad, but there is a fundamental difference between a tribute to an eighty-five-year-old grandparent who died in his sleep and a eulogy for a seven-year-old killed in an automobile accident or a thirty-nine-year-old mother felled by breast cancer.

When death follows a long, fulfilled life, a eulogy can be a way of celebrating as well as mourning. The death of a baby or child and accidental or untimely deaths call for different words. In such cases, even the consolation of memory seems impossible, since a whole life's worth of memories has been thwarted.

After a tragic death, an honest eulogy might tell the story of the tragedy. The rabbi or cantor should be given a full account of what happened, including the feelings of the survivors: anger at God, fear at what might happen next, bewilderment, numbness, despair. Support and assistance from family, friends, and community can be part of the story, too.

CLOSING: After the eulogy, the rabbi usually makes announcements about the burial (location of the cemetery, directions for the motorcade, etc.), about suggested charities for memorial donations, and about the family's plans for *shiva*, or "visitation."

The rabbi may add another short reading before the concluding prayer, *El Malei Rachamim*—"God Filled with Compassion." This is usually chanted or sung in Hebrew while the congregation stands.

God, whose fullness is compassion,
This One, dwelling on High.
Grant perfect peace under the wings of Your Presence,
In the holy and pure heights,
Like the heaven's radiant splendor,
To the soul of _____,
Daughter/son of _____,
Who has now gone on his/her way.

Let Eden be his/her portion.
Please O God of Compassion,
Protect him/her in the cover of Your presence forever.
May his/her soul be bound up in the bond of eternal life.
May God be his/her inheritance.
May he/she rest in peace.
And together we say,
Amen.[5]

RECESSIONAL: At the end of the service, pallbearers are called forward to carry the casket to the hearse. Carrying the casket (or wheeling the gurney that holds it) is considered a great honor, a final "gift." For children and grandchildren, carrying the coffin is a beautiful gesture of thanks to someone who once carried them.

According to *halachah*, only Jews can serve as pallbearers for other Jews, and traditionally the honor was given to the sons, grandsons, brothers, nephews, or cousins of the deceased. At liberal Jewish funerals, women serve as pallbearers, as do non-Jewish family members and close friends.

The casket leads the recessional out of the chapel, followed by the rabbi and the immediate family.[6] The motorcade to the cemetery is led by the hearse, followed by the family's cars, and then other guests and members of the congregation. People who attend a Jewish funeral service should make every effort to accompany the dead all the way to the cemetery, called the *bet ha-olam*—"eternal home."

Headlights and/or a windshield sticker identifies the motorcade as a funeral procession, to which other cars yield at streetlights. For large motorcades (more than ten or fifteen cars) the funeral home may suggest and arrange a police escort.

AT THE CEMETERY: The ceremony at the graveside includes a brief but powerful ritual of few words and powerful gestures.

According to Jewish custom, the casket is carried by the pallbearers from the hearse to the grave, followed by the rabbi and the immediate family. As a gesture of reticence at saying the last farewell, the procession moves slowly, and some rabbis make ritual stops on the way to the grave—three times or seven times, depending on local custom. The rabbi and/or cantor may recite a prayer or psalm while walking. Once everyone arrives at the grave, the casket is either placed on a bier above ground or immediately lowered into the earth.

GRAVESIDE LITURGY: The graveside service is not fixed by Jewish law. The order and selection of prayers vary according to community custom and rabbinical-cantorial preference. However, certain elements are nearly universal, brevity being chief among them.

If the funeral service took place in a chapel or synagogue, the graveside liturgy will include a few psalms, biblical readings, and/or short prayers. Among the more common readings are Psalm 90 ("Adonai, you have been a refuge in all generations"), Psalm 91 ("For God will bid the angels to you, to protect you upon all your paths"), and Ecclesiastes 3 ("To every thing there is a season"). If Psalm 23 ("The Lord is my Shepherd") was not recited before, it will certainly be read at the grave.

The traditional graveside prayer is the *Tzidduk Ha'din*— "Righteous Judgment." Like the blessing that concludes with the phrase *Dayan ha-Emet,* this prayer asserts that God knows what God is doing. (The Hebrew words *din* and *dayan* share a common root, which yields both "judgment" and "judge.") Many Jews are uncomfortable with this tribute to God's wisdom, especially in the aftermath of an untimely death. Most liberal rabbis omit it altogether, though some read it in Hebrew, without translation.[7]

Just as the eulogy is the liturgical heart of the funeral service, Kaddish is the emotional peak of the graveside ceremony. With this prayer, *aninut* ends and mourners begin the next period of grief, called *avelut.* As of this recitation, the mourners begin saying Kaddish for their loved one.

At more traditional funerals, the Burial Kaddish is recited. This prayer differs from the more familiar Mourner's Kaddish by expressing faith in God's intention to reestablish the Temple in Jerusalem and to raise the dead to everlasting life.[8]

The nearly universal substitution of the Mourner's Kaddish

for the Burial Kaddish is done not so much for theological reasons as for practical and compassionate ones. Few people know the Burial Kaddish and many are unable to read it. Even more important, however, is the emotional comfort embedded in the sounds and rhythms of the Mourner's Kaddish, which most Jews associate with grief and comfort even if they cannot read it or do not know the words by heart.

THE MOURNER'S KADDISH

יִתְגַּדַּל וְיִתְקַדַּשׁ שְׁמֵהּ רַבָּא בְּעָלְמָא דִּי בְרָא כִרְעוּתֵהּ
וְיַמְלִיךְ מַלְכוּתֵהּ בְּחַיֵּיכוֹן וּבְיוֹמֵיכוֹן וּבְחַיֵּי דְכָל בֵּית
יִשְׂרָאֵל בַּעֲגָלָא וּבִזְמַן קָרִיב וְאִמְרוּ אָמֵן:
יְהֵא שְׁמֵהּ רַבָּא מְבָרַךְ לְעָלַם וּלְעָלְמֵי עָלְמַיָּא:
יִתְבָּרַךְ וְיִשְׁתַּבַּח וְיִתְפָּאַר וְיִתְרוֹמַם וְיִתְנַשֵּׂא וְיִתְהַדָּר
וְיִתְעַלֶּה וְיִתְהַלָּל שְׁמֵהּ דְּקֻדְשָׁא בְּרִיךְ הוּא
לְעֵלָּא (לְעֵלָּא) מִן כָּל בִּרְכָתָא וְשִׁירָתָא תֻּשְׁבְּחָתָא וְנֶחֱמָתָא
דַּאֲמִירָן בְּעָלְמָא וְאִמְרוּ אָמֵן:
יְהֵא שְׁלָמָא רַבָּא מִן שְׁמַיָּא וְחַיִּים עָלֵינוּ וְעַל כָּל
יִשְׂרָאֵל וְאִמְרוּ אָמֵן:
עוֹשֶׂה שָׁלוֹם בִּמְרוֹמָיו הוּא יַעֲשֶׂה שָׁלוֹם עָלֵינוּ וְעַל
כָּל יִשְׂרָאֵל וְאִמְרוּ אָמֵן:

MOURNERS:*
Yit-ga-dal ve'yit-ka-dash sh'mei ra-ba

COMMUNITY:
Amen

MOURNERS:
B'alma di-ve-ra chir-u-tei v'yam-lich mal-chu-tei
b'chai-yei chon u-v-yo-mei-chon
u-v'chai-yei d'chol beit yis-ra-el

---

* *This "call and response" is common; however, sometimes the entire Kaddish is recited in unison.*

† *V'imru means "and say." This is an invitation to the community to join in for the "Amen."*

ba-a-ga-la u-viz-man ka-riv
V'im-ru†

MOURNERS AND COMMUNITY:
Amen
    Y'hei shmei ra-ba m'va-rach
    l'a-lam u-l'al-mei al-mai-ya

MOURNERS:
Yit-ba-rach v'yish-ta-bach
v'yit-pa-ar v'yit-ro-mam v'yit-na-sei
v'yit-ha-dar v'yit-a-leh v'yit-ha-lal
sh'mei d'ku-d'sha

MOURNERS AND COMMUNITY:
B'rich hu

MOURNERS:
L'ei-lah min kol bir-cha-ta v'shi-ra-ta
tush-b'cha-ta v'neh-cheh-ma-ta
da-a-mi-ran b'al-ma
V'im-ru

MOURNERS AND COMMUNITY:
Amen

MOURNERS:
Y'hei shla-ma ra-ba min sh'ma-ya
V'chay-yim a-lei-nu

v'al kol yis-ra-el
V'im-ru

MOURNERS AND COMMUNITY:
Amen

MOURNERS:
O-seh sha-lom bim-ro-mav hu ya-a-seh sha-lom
a-lei-nu v'al kol yis-ra-el
V'im-ru

MOURNERS AND COMMUNITY:
Amen

Exalted and hallowed be God's greatness
In this world of Your creation.
May Your will be fulfilled
And Your sovereignty revealed
And the life of the whole house of Israel
Speedily and soon.
And say, Amen.

May You be blessed forever,
Even to all eternity.
May You, most Holy One, be blessed,
Praised and honored, extolled and glorified,
Adored and exalted above all else.

Blessed are You.
Beyond all blessings and hymns, praises and consolations
That may be uttered in this world,
In the days of our lifetime,
And say, Amen.

May peace abundant descend from heaven
With life for us and for all Israel,
And say, Amen.

May God, Who makes peace on high,
Bring peace to all and to all Israel,
And say, Amen.

For a discussion of the history and meaning of Kaddish, see Chapter 1, "What Kaddish Means." Alternative translations and poems are found on pp. 202–212.

FILLING THE GRAVE: This is the most striking part of a Jewish funeral, surely the most painful, and perhaps ultimately the most healing.

Depending on the local custom, while the coffin is lowered into the earth, or just prior to filling the grave, the rabbi or cantor recites:

עַל מְקֹמוֹ יָבֹא בְשָׁלוֹם:
עַל מְקֹמָהּ תָּבֹא בְשָׁלוֹם:

Al mekomo yavo veshalom (for a man)
Al mekomah tavo veshalom (for a woman)

May _____ go to his/her place in peace.

The rabbi then hands one of the principal mourners a trowel or simply gestures for him or her to pick up the shovel placed beside or in a pile of newly dug earth. Children, parents, siblings, and spouse come forward, taking turns dropping a little of the soil onto the coffin.

According to one custom, mourners use the back of the shovel at first, to demonstrate reluctance. In some communities, each mourner replaces the shovel back in the earth rather than hand it from one person to the next—a practice probably born of the idea that death is somehow contagious. However, others find it comforting to give the spade to the next person, acknowledging the shared nature of the task. After the immediate family has symbolically buried their loved one, others come forward to take a turn with the shovel, thus completing the *mitzvah* of *levayah*.

ALTERNATIVES: Although many liberal Jews follow this tradition, some find it too painful. Sometimes mourners request that the coffin be delivered to the cemetery and placed into the grave before they arrive at the cemetery. Some families are uncomfortable with throwing dirt onto the coffin, especially when children are among the principle mourners, and drop flowers onto the coffin instead of earth.

Most rabbis gently try to dissuade mourners from leaving before the coffin is lowered, for both religious and psychological reasons. The idea of leaving the *mitzvah* of burial entirely in the hands of paid strangers deprives the family of its last act of *kevod ha-met,* respect for the dead. Even more important, helping to fill the grave means you have left nothing undone. The echo of earth falling on the wooden coffin is the terrible and haunting sound of finality. After you have emptied a shovel onto a loved one's casket, there is no denying death—which makes it possible for healing to begin.

RECESSIONAL: It is customary for the deceased's children, spouse, parents, and siblings to leave the graveside first. They walk past the rest of the community, which has arrayed itself into two rows—a gauntlet of loving, compassionate faces. Before or while the mourners walk down this aisle of loving faces, the rabbi may lead the group, phrase by phrase, in the traditional words of comfort:

הַמָּקוֹם יְנַחֵם אֶתְכֶם בְּתוֹךְ שְׁאָר אֲבֵלֵי צִיּוֹן
וִירוּשָׁלָיִם.

Ha-Ma-kom y'nach-em et-chem be-toch sh'ar a-va-lei Tzion
v'Ye-ru-sha-la-yim

May God comfort you among all the mourners of Zion
and Jerusalem.

This ritual marks the fundamental shift from the *mitzvah* of
kevod ha-met, honoring the dead, to *nichum avelim*, comforting
mourners.

HAND-WASHING: At Jewish cemeteries, a bucket of water
with a ladle or cup, will be set out for hand-washing. Everyone
present may participate in this ceremonial and symbolic act of
purification after coming into contact with death. No blessing is
recited as each person rinses both hands.

For Judaism, immersion in water often represents a change of
personal status. After the funeral, the mourner stops being an
onen and becomes an *avel*. This washing symbolizes the separation between the work of burying the dead and the work of
grieving for her.

Sometimes hand-washing is done at the *shiva* home rather
than at the cemetery. A basin and cup may be set out on the porch
or in the foyer for those who wish to wash after the burial. Other-
wise, mourners and guests who wish to wash can simply use a sink.

COST: Funerals are expensive. In addition to the cost of the casket, funeral homes charge for removal, storage and preparation of
the body, for limousine service, use of the funeral home chapel,
and a variety of extras, such as acknowledgment cards. Cemetery
fees (for opening and closing the grave, and for use of an on-site
chapel) are separate.

Traditional Jewish funerals—typified by *taharah* and a plain wooden coffin—tend to be more modest in price. But even the simplest funeral can cost several thousand dollars. If a family is unable to pay, state funds are generally available to cover the costs of a basic funeral.

PART III

COMPASSION
FOR THE
BEREAVED

Mom is dead. Regardless of her age or yours, you cry with a child's tears.

Your beloved is gone, the companion who laughed with you in health and who stayed near in sickness. The home you shared is silent as a stone.

How is it possible for a baby sister to die first? For a big brother to abandon you?

A beloved uncle, a best friend, a niece dies. No one understood you so well. No one acknowledges the depth of your loss.

The death of a child is monstrous, impossible to fathom. The future seems like a cruel joke.

To be "in mourning" is to inhabit a real place-in-time where "the valley of the shadow" is not just a metaphor but a parallel universe. In mourning, the world looks and feels unfamiliar. What was once ordinary seems frightening.

In mourning, grief is the color of the sky, the taste of bread, and the temperature of the body. Grief is also the task at hand: facing the newly empty world and learning how to live in it. This is hard work, exhausting work.

The Jewish mourner has a well-marked path through this dark, difficult place-in-time. The ancient rituals and customs anticipate most contemporary theories about bereavement and provide tools for the work of grief: words to name the unutterable pain, sacred obligations—*mitzvot*—to give shape to hollow days.

....

CHAPTER SIX

THE LANDSCAPE
OF MOURNING

GRIEF

Grief is the way that bereaved people heal. And heal they can. Mourners can come to terms with loss, develop a new relationship to the loved one who has died, and learn how to live in the world again. Pain gives way to equilibrium, and while life never returns to what it was before, new definitions of normalcy emerge. Sometimes, grief even leads to personal growth, transforming the mourner into a more compassionate human being.

Grief is no abstraction. It is as tangible as granite. It can feel like a heavy weight on the shoulders or in the chest. Grief can cause weakness, and physical exhaustion. The list of symptoms associated with grief includes headaches, dizziness, nausea, dry mouth, and intestinal problems. Sleep disorders and fatigue are common. Some people lose their appetite, some become accident-prone, many find themselves oversensitive to light or noise. Symptoms usually subside within a month or two, although they sometimes recur around holidays or anniversaries.

Mourners often say they feel like they're going crazy, but while everyone who grieves feels depressed, few mourners actually cross the line into clinical depression. Nevertheless, if symptoms such as crushing fatigue, insomnia, loss of appetite, or an inability to go out of the house persist for months, it is wise to seek help from a sensitive rabbi and/or a therapist with training and experience with bereavement. (See below, "Taking Comfort.")

The emotional and psychological impact of grief has been studied, dissected, and diagrammed. The most familiar theories about grief suggest that people follow a pattern, moving from denial to acceptance in a more or less predictable sequence.[1] The other common view treats grief as a kind of acute disease that can be "cured," mostly by the passage of time.

But both of these paradigms tend to make grief into a passive, almost involuntary process. Time alone does not "heal all wounds" automatically. Recovering from the trauma of a loss can take as much effort as learning to walk after the amputation of a leg— except that no one can see the magnitude of your adjustment.

Death brings up different feelings and issues for everyone. There may be anger at the deceased, at other people, at God, or fate; guilt for terrible things said to the deceased and guilt for things that were never said, and even guilt for still being alive; fear of loneliness and fear of death; bottomless sadness.

Some people express their feelings with rivers of tears, some in withdrawn silence. Whatever the form, grief takes time and patience. There is no uniform timetable for this work nor is there any way to short-circuit it. It takes as long as you need.

THE JEWISH VIEW OF GRIEF: Jewish tradition takes a typically task-oriented approach to grief, asking mourners and their communities to perform *mitzvot*. Virtually from the moment a death occurs, mourners are asked to *do* things that both honor the dead and keep them connected to the living.

Most people find that knowing what they are "supposed" to do next works like an anchor during the emotional storms that follow a death. As the days pass, Jewish mourners participate in rituals that give shape to the emotional chaos and break through the terrible isolation of bereavement. Jewish rituals and customs provide a kind of itinerary of grief work, carving out time for weeping, remembering, and learning, for looking inward and for reaching out.

For example, *shiva*, the seven-day period that follows the funeral, is a time and place for facing the full impact of death, supported by family and loving friends. When this period ends, the mourner leaves the private sanctuary of *shiva* to take up the responsibilities of family and work within the protective confines of *shloshim*, the "thirty days."

The mourner is not, however, rushed to "get over" the pain and get on with life. Tradition mandates keeping some distance from frivolity: going to work but avoiding office parties; attending a family bar mitzvah but not the reception that follows. After the first month, mourners are given the task of saying Kaddish with others, acknowledging the ongoing process of grief within a communal setting.

Judaism places protective fences around grief. Barriers of time and ritual shield the mourner, permitting him or her to do what must be done: weep, rant, rest. But the fences also protect against the excesses of grief; to keep sadness from overwhelming the life of the mourner, to keep death from impinging on the life of the community. The boundaries around mourning rituals become less and less restrictive over time so mourners can fully return to their life-affirming responsibilities: caring for themselves and their families materially and emotionally, repairing the world, participating in community life.

Indeed, the sanctity and joy of life are such paramount Jewish values, if any protective "fence" poses a threat to the health or even to the livelihood of a mourner, he or she is permitted and even obliged to ignore it. Life always takes precedence over death. If a funeral processional and a wedding processional meet at a crossroads, it is the bridal party that has the right of way.

The Jewish emphasis on life explains why the status of "official mourner" is limited to immediate family members: father and mother, husband and wife, brother and sister, son and daughter. All eight of these relatives are obligated, by Jewish law, to obey the rules of mourning for the first thirty days. After that, only children of the deceased are required to continue saying Kaddish for a year (eleven or twelve months, depending on custom).

The rabbis who codified Jewish law made the circle of official mourners small to keep death from overwhelming life. When pneumonia was a fatal illness and infant mortality common, this was a practical and compassionate choice. "When a man indulges in excessive grief for his dead, he will soon find himself weeping for another dead."[2]

Today, however, some of the traditional fences can seem insensitive rather than compassionate. For example, until recently, Jewish parents of babies who died in the first month of life were discouraged (and even prohibited) from having a funeral, much less sitting *shiva*. Today, the prohibition is gone as the Jewish community has begun to embrace what bereavement counselors call "disenfranchised mourners."

Like the bereaved parents of babies stillborn or even miscarried, many mourners go unacknowledged and unattended. In addition to extended family members such as in-laws, uncles, aunts, and cousins, close friends generally have no "status" as mourners. Gay and lesbian partners are often themselves cut off from the comforts of ritual and the support of community. Jews-by-choice may be at a loss when mourning for members of their non-Jewish family. And in the name of "protecting" them from sadness, children's grief can be overlooked or denied.

Rabbis and funeral directors have grown increasingly attentive to mourners outside the nuclear family, and the ritual comforts of Jewish tradition are certainly available to anyone who feels shattered by death. People who identify themselves as bereaved can attend services to say Kaddish, or wear the torn ribbon (*k'riah,* explained in Chapter 5), or light a memorial candle. Any synagogue member can request bereavement counseling from his or her rabbi.

FAMILY CONFLICT

"My father was not a religious man, and he said he didn't want any rabbis or prayers at his funeral. But it's so important to me and to my kids that our rabbi be there with us."

"My mother wanted to be cremated and have her ashes scattered in the mountains. She made me promise again and again that I'd honor her wish. But I want to bury her as a Jew, sit *shiva,* and put up a stone at her grave."

"My Orthodox brother refuses to go to our sister's funeral if a woman rabbi conducts the service. This rabbi was her dear friend! What are we going to do?

"My mother told me she wanted a 'traditional' funeral with flowers and organ music. But now I know that these aren't traditional and my rabbi tells me they aren't even permitted in our synagogue."

Death often brings families together: extended families scattered around the world gather to mourn; brothers and sisters long at odds find common ground in their grief. But sometimes, funerals are scenes of family tension and dissent. Reunions at the graveside or during *shiva* can expose or reignite profound disagreements. Decisions about how to bury and mourn a loved one and about how to interpret or observe Jewish ritual can become flash points, especially since these choices must be made quickly.

Deathbed wishes and promises sometimes pose serious dilemmas; a parent's expressed request for cremation, for example, can be very painful for a son or daughter who feels torn between filial loyalty and the wish to follow Jewish custom. A wife who "forbids" her husband to sit *shiva* may be cutting him off from solace and support.

Rabbis and funeral directors have experience with such conundrums and may be able to offer guidance or even suggest a compromise. For example, a funeral with flowers and organ music might be held in a funeral chapel rather than the synagogue. The woman rabbi might offer the eulogy but step aside and let the brother lead Kaddish. For most liberal Jews, cremation doesn't mean that the family can't sit *shiva* or perform other traditional *mitzvot*.

Presented with these kinds of problems, Jewish law tends to side with the need to comfort the bereaved. According to *halachah*, survivors may ignore explicit requests not to be mourned with Jewish ritual.[3]

TAKING COMFORT

All mourners deserve support, guidance, and comfort. Synagogue members will find these within their congregations, though only if they reach out and when they accept help. Jews who feel cut off from Judaism can also find compassion and assistance in the Jewish community. It's a matter of seeking it out.

RABBIS AND CANTORS: For many clergy, helping the sick and bereaved are their finest pastoral hours. Rabbis and cantors who have been present at death and comforted mourners in its immediate aftermath invariably speak of the great privilege of being present at these terrible yet holy moments. Mourners often report feeling closer to their clergy having shared these experiences with them. Of course, like all other human beings the clergy bring strengths and weaknesses to death and mourning and there are stories about abrupt and unfeeling rabbis and cantors. But, for the most part, they are enormously helpful when death comes.

Synagogue members should let their rabbi know if a loved one is gravely ill or near death. Do not assume that he or she will be automatically informed of all hospitalizations or illnesses within the congregation. Rabbis do not get calls from hospitals; the only way they can help is if they are told when help is needed.

If a final illness or death occurs in-town, your rabbi and/or your loved one's rabbi will probably visit, stay in touch by phone, alert others in the synagogue, and generally provide whatever support and assistance he or she can. Sometimes, the rabbi's schedule may prevent him or her from visiting as much as either of you would like, but most do everything they can to be present in times of crisis.

Call the synagogue, even if a final illness or death occurs out of town. When you return home, the rabbi and/or cantor should meet with you to offer condolences and perhaps discuss holding a memorial or *shiva* service that will enable you to mourn with your own community. Given the geographical dispersion of so many families, this is common practice.

Rabbis cannot change long-standing family dynamics, nor can they take away the fear of death or the pain of grief. They can, however, bear witness to struggle in the same "ministry of presence" that is so important to the dying.

The rabbi is both a real and a symbolic connection to Jewish tradition and the Jewish community. Many rabbis report that as death approaches, people who never considered themselves religious or spiritual express a need to talk about God, Judaism, or the afterlife. Clergy will gladly talk about anything that a dying person or his family wishes to discuss. The rabbi may offer to pray or chant, or help those at the deathbed say their final good-byes—as the family wishes.

After a death, your rabbi or cantor may come to the hospital or to your home. He or she will pray with you, read psalms, answer questions, or just stay beside you, as you wish. Clergy are familiar with local funeral homes, cemeteries, and support services, and are a great source of practical information as well as emotional support.

In the face of death, many people without affiliation or synagogue membership find themselves longing for a communal and/or spiritual connection. Even if you or your loved one are not "believers," even if neither of you has belonged to a synagogue for years, you should be able to find a sympathetic rabbi. In some cities and towns, the Jewish community supports hospice rabbis who specialize in the needs of the dying and their families. (See below.) Funeral home staff, hospital chaplains, and the local Jewish Family and Children's Service are all sources for referral to local rabbis.

PAYMENT: There is no charge for the clergy's services to synagogue members; however, it is customary to make a donation to the rabbi's discretionary fund, or to another congregational charity, such as the temple library. Unaffiliated mourners who use the services of a rabbi or cantor (usually recommended by a funeral home director) are responsible for a separate honorarium for the clergy. In cases of financial need, the fee is usually waived.

HOSPITAL CHAPLAINS: A self-selected group of caregivers who work without high-tech tools or any assurance that they can "fix things," hospital chaplains can provide both comfort and practical information. The chaplain's job has less to do with prayer or religious instruction than with just being present for people who are suffering and to listen to people's stories.

Non-Jewish chaplains will generally refer Jewish patients and families to a local rabbi. If that is not possible, they will make themselves available, and since most are trained in the beliefs and customs of all major religions, they are usually able to answer basic questions about Jewish funeral homes and mourning customs. It is completely inappropriate (and very rare) for chaplains to preach or teach their own beliefs to anyone of a different faith.

HOSPICE: The hospice movement provides palliative medical care to the dying. Although there are residential hospices, most programs support families in their efforts to keep dying loved ones at home. Rabbis are virtually unanimous in recommending hospice services when it is clear that death is imminent.

Hospice workers—nurses, aides, social workers, physicians—can be of enormous assistance to the dying person and to his or her family in countless practical ways, from giving pain medication to locating meals-on-wheels programs. They are also models of compassion who demonstrate how to be present for the dying. Having watched many funeral directors, bereavement counselors, and clergy with the dying and bereaved, hospice workers are also a good source for referrals. Local hospice programs often run bereavement groups.

Jewish hospice does not duplicate the medical services provided by nonsectarian hospices. Instead, it provides spiritual and communal support by sending rabbis or trained lay people to visit individuals and families who seek their services.

Jewish hospice rabbis and staff are specialists in pastoral care, with a wealth of experience in end-of-life issues. They can talk about the tradition's view of death, answer questions about Jewish views of the afterlife, or pray at the bedside. In all they do, Jewish hospice workers are guided by the wishes of the dying person and his or her family.

Some requests for Jewish hospice come from families that are disconnected from the community, but synagogue members also use these services. There is no such thing as too much compassion for the dying or for their loved ones.

Jewish hospice programs are generally supported by local Jewish federations and work under the auspices of an agency or organization, such as the local Jewish Family and Children's Service or a Jewish Healing Center. The National Institute for Jewish Hospice can also provide referrals to local services. (See "Bibliography and Resources.")

FUNERAL HOME STAFF: If funeral arrangements were made in advance, contact with the funeral director may entail little more than a phone call or two. But in the absence of what is called a "pre-need contract," mourners may spend a good deal of time speaking to funeral home staff. For some Jews, the person who answers the phone at the funeral home is their first contact with the Jewish community in many years.

On a practical level, funeral directors or counselors explain the mourner's choice of services and goods related to preparation of the body and funeral services. Mortuary staff can also do everything from locating a rabbi to placing the obituary to setting up chairs for *shiva*. The Federal Trade Commission requires full disclosure of all available options, services, fees, as well as any relevant regulations or laws.[4]

But the exemplars of the profession are more than just businesspeople. Some funeral directors are wonderful teachers who try to live up to the ideals of the traditional *hevra kadisha*, the holy burial society, and help mourners understand their Jewish choices. They explain the rituals and laws and provide informational pamphlets, bibliographies, and lists of local bereavement resources. There is also a movement in the funeral industry to provide more comprehensive "aftercare" for the bereaved, including support groups, counseling, and referrals to local therapists.

Cities with sizable Jewish populations generally have more than one Jewish funeral home. They are all profit-making companies, owned by local families or by national chains. Some are enormous, some are intimate. If you find yourself in a position of having to select one, seek a recommendation from a rabbi, friend, or even a hospital chaplain or nurse.

Jewish funeral homes are accustomed to diversity within the Jewish community and tend to be nonjudgmental. So while any

Jewish funeral home can serve strictly observant Jews by honoring all of the laws pertaining to the preparation of the body, most will also arrange for embalming or cremation (which are forbidden by Jewish law) if that is the family's wish.

In smaller cities and towns, there may be only one or two nonsectarian funeral homes to serve the whole community. These businesses maintain good relationships with local rabbis and tend to be respectful of Jewish laws and customs. If members of the Jewish community wish to prepare the body for burial in the traditional manner—washing and dressing it in simple white shrouds—the funeral home will usually make its facilities available. The more explicit mourners can be in their directions, the better the funeral director can honor their wishes.

SYNAGOGUE RESOURCES: Most congregations do their best to help people in times of grave illness and bereavement. When the rabbi or synagogue office is informed about a death, the appropriate individuals and committees are alerted.

Committees that assist members in times of need go by a variety of names and carry different briefs. "Caring Community" may help with everything from driving people to medical appointments, to preparing food for the gathering after the funeral. The "Condolence Committee" may be charged with setting up *shiva minyans*. "*Bikkur Holim*" (visiting the sick), usually organizes hospital and home visits. "*Gemilut Hasadim*" (acts of loving-kindness) may visit the sick and also assist families who have suffered a recent loss.

Some *hevra kadisha* committees prepare a congregational funeral package for members, hold seminars about death and mourning rituals, and/or run *shiva* services for mourners in their homes. In a small but growing number of liberal congregations, the *hevra kadisha* actually prepares bodies for burial in the traditional manner, washing and dressing them in simple white shrouds.[5] (See Chapter 3.)

For the most part, however, synagogue committees tend to focus on the needs of the bereaved. Committee members deliver food to the home following the funeral and/or provide meals during *shiva*. They may offer to make phone calls, drive out-of-town funeralgoers to and from the airport, run errands, take over car-pool duties, or provide baby-sitting for young children.

Some mourners are overwhelmed by the offers to help and are reluctant to accept. But saying yes is actually a good deed in its own right. People who volunteer to visit the sick, care for the dead, or comfort mourners report that performing these *mitzvot* is not a burden but an honor.

HEALING SERVICES: For many people, the term "healing service" calls to mind fundamentalist television evangelists who purport to work miraculous cures upon true believers. Jewish healing services could not be more different.[6] Comprised of heartfelt readings, quiet singing or chanting, prayers, and silent meditation, healing services provide time to acknowledge the continuing pain of loss, to remember, reflect, and forge ties with others.

Jewish healing services focus on prayers for wholeness, or *shleymut*, and healing of the spirit, or *refuat hanefesh*. Sometimes held on a weeknight, sometimes folded into a regular Sabbath service, they offer fellowship, meditation, and prayer for people who are battling or recovering from serious illness, caring for a sick loved one, or are going through a divorce or other family difficulty. Mourners at various stages of bereavement also attend, and the Mourners' Kaddish is invariably part of the liturgy.

Healing services are a growing phenomenon in synagogues around the country. The National Center for Jewish Healing publishes a pamphlet that describes the content and nature of such services, and is a resource for people interested in writing their own.[7] (See "Bibliography and Resources.")

BEREAVEMENT GROUPS: Even with a loving family, a caring community, and a wise rabbi, some mourners cannot break through the isolation of grief. Bereavement groups provide a kind of fellowship and support founded on shared experience and understanding. In bereavement groups, widows and widowers discover that it's not crazy or evil to feel angry at the spouse who "abandoned them." Groups help mourners explore the wide range of normal grieving and share strategies for relearning how to live in the world. People who meet in these groups sometimes form lasting friendships.

There are all kinds of bereavement groups—from highly organized to very informal. Community-sponsored or synagogue-based bereavement groups are usually conducted by social workers or psychologists for a set number of sessions. Open-ended support groups meet to help people coping with specific kinds of losses, such as death due to violence, or suicide; these may be facilitated by a peer member. There are also one-time workshops on specific topics, such as "Cooking for One," or "The First Passover Without Your Loved One."

Bereavement groups are led by all kinds of agencies and organizations, both secular and Jewish: hospice organizations, community centers, senior centers, synagogues, funeral homes, and Jewish Family and Children's Services.

It may take years before a mourner is ready for a bereavement group. Grief can pay a "visit" even long after the official mourning periods are over, and these groups are open to mourners at any time.

Although many people find that the support and fellowship of a bereavement group provides all the counseling they need, groups cannot always devote the time necessary to address underlying personal problems raised by the death of a loved one. Counseling or therapy (the terms are used interchangeably) can be an intimate platform not only for healing, but also for personal growth.

COUNSELING: Though grief is not mental illness, the emotions that attend it can be frightening, the issues it raises profoundly disturbing. The loss of a parent or sibling can prompt a mourner to reexamine the family's history and delve into childhood issues. Losing a spouse may start a complete life review. For parents who lose children, therapy is often part of learning to live with the pain. Mourners may not be ready to grapple with such difficult subjects in the immediate aftermath of a death, but seek help after a year or even many years later.

If symptoms of depression persist for months and/or get in the way of daily functioning, it's a good idea to seek professional help. For people who are very isolated in their grief—who have little or no community support or feel unable to talk freely to family or friends—therapy is sometimes the only safe place to give voice to grief. But even without "symptoms," and even when surrounded by family and friends, individual counseling can be a personal watershed.

Therapists can be social workers, psychologists, or psychiatrists. Regardless of their credentials, not all therapists are equally prepared to help the bereaved. While all counselors help their patients cope with losses, there are special skills and talents that are particularly relevant to mourners.

The best place to start looking for a therapist to help cope with grief is to ask people you know and trust, such as your rabbi or physician. Recently bereaved friends may have recommendations worth heeding. If there is a Jewish Healing Center or Jewish hospice rabbi in your community, call and ask if they provide individual counseling or can make a referral.

At your first session with a therapist, ask if he or she is comfortable talking about death and grief, or has taken courses in the field. Inquire if he or she is a member of the Association for Death Education and Counseling. Trust your instincts; if you feel uncomfortable talking to one counselor, look for someone else.

BOOKS: Seeking comfort from the pages of a book is a time-honored Jewish custom. During the first weeks and months after a death, it is traditional to read books about Jewish mourning customs and the biblical literature of sorrow and comfort, which includes the books of Job, Lamentations, and Psalms. In the aftermath of a death, readers usually do not look to books for pleasure or even distraction, but follow the rabbinic adage, "At the time when one should be joyous—be joyous. And when it is time to mourn—mourn."[8]

Some people read books that were treasured by the person who died. Reading aloud to children—especially books geared to helping them grieve—can be a boon to both bereaved child and bereaved adult.

Lately, grief has become something of a best-seller. Since the publication of Elisabeth Kübler-Ross's book *On Death and Dying* in 1969, countless volumes about death and mourning have appeared, with titles that address every kind of loss. There are books about death due to cancer, to suicide, to AIDS, and to violence; books geared to the concerns of widows, teenagers, and young children, and more general treatments of bereavement.

The Jewish literature about grief is extensive and growing, too. Jewish titles run the gamut from simple question-and-answer-style pamphlets about planning a funeral to scholarly tomes about the afterlife. There are many bibliographies on the subject of death and mourning—including the one at the end of this book. (See "Bibliography and Resources.")

....

CHAPTER SEVEN

SHIVA:
THE SEVEN DAYS

SHIVA, BASED ON THE HEBREW WORD FOR SEVEN (*SHEVA*) is a protected island in time for the bereaved. It begins immediately after the funeral and is a seven-day period of withdrawal from the world to foster the difficult but healing work of grief.

The phrase "sitting *shiva*" probably derives from the custom of sitting low to the ground during the intense period of mourning after the funeral. Mourners do not sit still for seven days; they move around the house, stand, sit at the table to eat, lie down to sleep. And yet, the image of sitting during *shiva*—of motionlessness—is an apt metaphor for what happens over the course of this week. During *shiva*, mourners *sit with* their grief, remembering, weeping, dreaming, telling stories, sharing memories. Although it may be a quiet time, sitting *shiva* is not passive.

During the week, mourners are exempt from all the requirements of daily life and restricted from its pleasures, too. The bereaved do not work or play, call the office or wash dishes, watch TV or go to the gym. *Shiva* is for one thing only, and that is exploring the emotional catalog of grief: sorrow, emptiness, regret, relief, guilt, anger, shame, self-pity, remorse.

Every *shiva* is difficult in its own way. Sometimes the bitterness of loss is tempered by the sweetness of memory; when death follows a long, productive life, reflecting upon the past can be a source of tangible blessings. But there are other times when *shiva* is little more than a blind cave; a child dies or a husband is killed and the agony is breathtaking. And sometimes *shiva* feels razoredged; how does one grieve for an abusive parent, an estranged sibling, an unreconciled child?

Whatever the details, the weight of grief can be overwhelming. Thus, *shiva* supplies communal support, morning and evening, day in and day out. The presence of family members, friends, and neighbors makes the burden more bearable.

Shiva works best when mourners understand the hows and whys of the ritual, and when the bereaved are members of a community that knows how to care for them. Which is why some liberal Jews forgo *shiva*.

The weeklong ritual raises a host of choices about how to be Jewish and how Jewish to be. Should we cover the mirrors? Do we really want a lot of people in the house after Mom's death? How many days should we sit? We don't belong to a temple, so, since none of us read Hebrew, who would lead services? How can I be comforted when all my friends live thousands of miles from where the rest of my family is sitting *shiva*?

The following pages describe the full complement of *shiva* customs. American Jews tend to choose from among the traditions based on what they find meaningful and practicable: for example, covering mirrors but wearing shoes in the house, or holding *shiva minyans* on three evenings rather than morning and evening all week. The key is to remember the purpose of *shiva*—which is to permit grieving to begin.

WHO SITS *SHIVA*: Jewish law requires that the immediate family spend this week in formal mourning. This includes adult children, parents, siblings, and spouses only. However, other relatives and friends sometimes join for some or all of its observance.

COUNTING THE DAYS: Seven is a mystical number in most religious traditions. In the biblical account of creation, the world was created in seven days and in a sense begins again every seven days. Every human death diminishes the world by the same measure. The Jewish custom of mourning for seven days is based on the verse in Genesis where Joseph mourns his father Jacob for a week.[1]

Though seven days may sound like a long time to "sit," in practice the seven are more like five because fractions of days are considered full days. Thus, the day of the funeral is counted as the first day of *shiva*, even if the burial occurred in the afternoon. Likewise, *shiva* ends on the morning of the seventh day—traditionally, right after *shacharit*, the morning prayer service.

Jewish tradition acknowledges the difference between the first three days of *shiva*, when grief tends to be overwhelming, and the remainder of the week, as mourners begin to face the future.[2] When people make a conscious decision to shorten their observance of *shiva*, it is usually to three days.

There are many reasons why people shorten *shiva*. Parents with young or school-aged children may need to attend to their families, especially if *shiva* is held out of town. If the death followed a long illness, weeks or months of anticipatory grief can make seven days feel excessive. Some professional obligations cannot be put off, especially if other people's needs are at risk. The rabbis understood this when they exempted physicians whose patients might suffer from their absence. But they also advised that mourners try to find substitutes and/or postpone leaving until after the third day at least. (In contemporary practice, this might mean going into the office for a few hours on the fourth or fifth day only for as long as it takes to clear up pressing business.)

Rabbis, bereavement counselors, and experienced mourners all counsel against shortening *shiva*. The first days give family members time to cry and share their feelings. As the week wears on, it becomes more appropriate to talk about realities such as when to go through the house or apartment, or when to read the will.

WHAT *SHIVA* LOOKS LIKE: *Shiva* is traditionally observed either in the home of the deceased or in the home of a principal mourner. If possible, mourners spend the whole week in the *shiva* house together, sleeping under the same roof. Where this is not practical, mourners share their waking hours.

Just as *shiva* transforms how mourners pass time, it also changes the look and use of space.

- Sitting low to the ground—on the floor, on cushions, or special benches provided by the funeral home—is an outward sign of being struck down by grief. (Visitors sit on regular chairs and couches.)
- The practice of covering the mirrors began centuries ago and was based on a belief that spirits were attracted to mirrors. Some people thought that the soul could be trapped in the reflection, or that the dead person's spirit lingered on earth for a time and might reach out from

"the other side." The rabbis reinterpreted the folk custom, declaring that mirrors should be covered to discourage vanity and encourage inner reflection. Regardless of its symbolism, covering mirrors is a striking visual cue, a token of the disruption and grief felt by everyone who enters the house.

- Doors are left unlocked so that visitors can enter without knocking or ringing the doorbell, which would distract the mourners from their grief and cause them to act as hosts.

- A condolence book (often provided by the funeral home) may be set out in a prominent spot. This can be a useful record if family members wish to write thank-you notes to visitors. Condolence books and thank-you notes are American secular and Christian customs that have been adopted by many Jews. Though traditionally one would never thank someone (or expect to be thanked) for fulfilling a *mitzvah* as profound as honoring the dead or comforting the bereaved, many people find that writing to visitors and answering sympathy cards are part of the healing process.

- Other common objects in a *shiva* home include a seven-day memorial candle, and prayer books for *minyan* services. Jewish funeral homes or your synagogue will generally provide these in a *shiva* "kit" that might also include low benches or chairs, folding chairs for guests, and *yarmulkes*.

BEGINNING: *Shiva* starts when the mourners return home from the funeral. The rituals are elemental, and for the most part, wordless.

- Shoes: Mourners remove their shoes and refrain from wearing leather shoes—an ancient sign of luxury—while in the *shiva* house. Wearing cloth slippers, socks, or going barefoot is a sign of being humbled by loss.

- Water: A basin of water and a towel may be left outside the door for people to wash their hands, a ritual gesture that separates the *mitzvah* of honoring the dead from the *mitzvah* of comforting the bereaved. (This is usually done at the cemetery, as described in Chapter 5.)

- Light: It is customary to light a large *shiva* candle, also called a *ner daluk*—burning light—which burns for seven days and nights. Candles are universal symbols of the divine spark that inhabits the body. In the words of the Bible, "The soul is the lamp of God."[3] The candle is placed in a prominent spot and lit without saying a blessing. The immediate family might gather and designate someone to light the flame; this honor can go to a child, close friend, or other "unofficial" mourner. The funeral home provides a long-burning candle or a special electric light that stays lit throughout *shiva*.

- Food: Serving a meal to mourners upon their return from the cemetery is a tangible act of condolence. Although the bereaved tend to be uninterested in eating, friends provide nourishment to signal that life must go on.

In the *Shulchan Aruch,* a sixteenth-century guide to Jewish law, Rabbi Joseph Karo wrote, "The first meal eaten by the mourner after the funeral is called *seudat havra'ah*, the meal of recuperation. At this meal, the mourner is forbidden to eat of his own food. It is a *mitzvah* for friends and neighbors to bring him food. The custom is to include round cakes or eggs in the meal of recuperation."[4]

Rabbi Karo's suggested menu of round foods recalls the cyclical nature of life, thus lentil dishes are traditional. Bread, the most elemental of foods, is always served. The meal is usually nonmeat, or *milchig* (dairy). It may be provided and served by a synagogue bereavement committee, or by friends and neighbors.

The meal usually begins with the blessing over bread, the *motzi.*

It is customary for people who attend the funeral and burial to return to the *shiva* house and share this meal with the bereaved. At some point during the funeral, the rabbi will announce, "You are all invited back to the Cohen home for the *seudat havra'ah,* the meal of consolation."

This is usually the largest gathering in the *shiva* house, and many mourners are deeply moved and comforted by the presence of many people. Sometimes, however, the *seudat havra'ah* can get out of hand. Too many people standing around eating and making small talk can turn it into a kind of Jewish wake. The mood and tone of *shiva* should be subdued—especially during the first hours. In some communities, guests serve the mourners and then leave them alone to eat.

If the funeral is very large and/or the family wishes a more intimate gathering, mourners can limit the size of the *seudat havra'ah* by personally inviting only a small group of close friends and asking the rabbi to make a different kind of announcement during the funeral. For example, "The family will be sitting *shiva* until Wednesday and invites you to come by anytime after tonight." Or "Visitation will be from six to nine P.M. Tuesday and Thursday."

During the rest of *shiva,* friends, neighbors, and synagogue bereavement committees continue to bring food and set up refreshments after services. Whether or not the family observes the Jewish dietary laws, it's best to prepare vegetarian or dairy dishes, or have meals delivered by a kosher restaurant or caterer; that way, family members and friends who do keep kosher will be able to eat.

Bereaved families often receive far more food than they can use or freeze, and it is a good idea to call before bringing yet another casserole or plate of brownies. Friends and neighbors can help dispose of any surplus by taking food to a local soup kitchen. The seemingly elemental urge to feed mourners can be turned into an act of charity honor by making a donation to a local food pantry or to Mazon: A Jewish Response to Hunger.[5]

HOW TO SIT *SHIVA*: After the rush of preparing for the funeral, the catharsis of the burial, and the communal outpouring of the *seudat havra'ah,* the rest of *shiva* can seem like a dark, lonely tunnel.

Jewish law is very specific about the prohibitions given to mourners. The bereaved do not cook, or run errands, or attend school. They do not wear makeup or shave. Mourners abstain from pleasures of all kinds: sensual, sexual, or even intellectual. Mourners are not supposed to read the Torah, which is considered one of life's great joys. Distractions are not permitted: so no television, card-playing, shopping, or computer games.[6]

This kind of self-denial is usually explained as an aide to grieving. However, there may well be a penitential aspect to some of the prohibitions and customs. Regardless of how much the deceased was loved and how complete the reconciliation at the time of death, mourners may be feeling anger, relief, or regret as well as sadness; for these, the relatively modest privations of *shiva* make a kind of restitution.

But *shiva* is more than a list of don'ts. There are many ways to "sit with" grief:

Remember: *Shiva* is, above all, a time for reminiscence. Telling and trading stories about the deceased is one of the primary activities of the week. At first, the stories may focus on the final illness, death, and the funeral. As the days pass, the story usually shifts to earlier, healthier memories of the loved one. Favorite anecdotes will be repeated, long-forgotten memories will be recalled. Family members compare different versions of the same story, which will be repeated for visitors, over and over again. Displaying albums or photographs of the deceased is a good way to elicit questions from visitors, who may or may not have known him. Inevitably, someone will say, "If only Dad were here; he would have loved seeing us all together like this!"

No emotions are out of bounds during *shiva*. Some anecdotes may bring on tears, but others will generate laughter. There is nothing wrong or inappropriate about laughing in a house of mourning. It is part of how mourners reclaim the memory of the whole person who died—including his sense of humor, her favorite jokes. Laughter can be part of the bereaved's ongoing relationship with the deceased.

Reminiscing and condolence also takes place on the phone and through e-mail, especially for people sitting *shiva* far from their own homes.

Friends and neighbors come and go, providing mourners with opportunities to remember and tell stories. But inevitably, there will be hours when nobody comes by and the family is talked out.

Some of the following suggestions—walking and listening to music—depart from traditional observance, but some mourners find them consistent with the spirit and purpose of *shiva*.

Read: Mourners often find it very difficult to concentrate on the printed page at the beginning of the week. As the days pass, however, many people look for something to read. Some study Jewish mourning customs; others prefer inspirational writings or poetry. Visitors may bring books they found helpful when they lost a loved one. If several people are reading together, you can share passages and read them aloud.

Write in a journal (a *shiva* journal can be a thoughtful gift from a friend). This can be as basic as listing the names of people who visited or called, or a chronicle of emotions, hour to hour, day by day. Record conversations with visitors and the memories they shared. Write a letter to the deceased.

Look at photo albums or home movies and videos.

Pray or meditate.

Walk: Taking a leisurely walk around the neighborhood, either alone or in quiet conversation with a family member or friend, can help memories flow. A well-known meditation practice, walking also relieves the inevitable claustrophobia and frayed nerves of staying inside with family members who are in pain, too.

Listen: Listening to music during *shiva* is prohibited by Jewish law because music is associated with happiness or used for distraction. But many people use music to focus on their grief. Listening to a loved one's favorite song or symphony can be comforting, or painful, or both.

Rest: Whatever mourners do during *shiva*—however little it may seem—the days are exhausting. Remember that grief takes a physical toll. Be kind to yourself. Rest. If possible, nap. When trying to rest, let would-be visitors know by leaving a note on the door and a message on the answering machine.

PRAYER SERVICES—*SHIVA MINYANS*: According to Jewish law, mourners are required to recite Kaddish daily in memory of the dead. However, since Kaddish may only be recited with a *minyan*—a prayer quorum of ten adult Jews—and since mourners were traditionally prohibited from leaving their homes, the synagogue comes to the mourner.

Kaddish is part of the weekday prayer service, which is held both morning (*shacharit*) and evening (*mincha/ma'ariv*)* in traditional synagogues. (Liberal congregations sometimes hold weekday services once a day. See Chapter 8.)

People who are not regular synagogue-goers or who are unfamiliar with weekday prayers may be intimidated by the idea of holding service in their homes. However, mourners do not lead these sessions. Sometimes, rabbis and cantors lead the *shiva minyan*, but it may be led by any Jew who knows the prayers.

The *shiva minyan* prays the regular weekday service (with a few modifications)[7] found in every *siddur*, or prayer book. The funeral home loans out prayer booklets, which come in the typical *shiva* "kit" along with folding chairs and *kippot* (Hebrew for yarmulkes). If you expect a lot of guests, make sure to ask for extra copies. Some synagogues provide their own *shiva* prayer books.

Mourners can choose to hold one or two services daily. Morning *minyans* tend to take place early—7 or 7:30 A.M.—so that people can get to work. The service is about thirty minutes

---

* *Technically, prayers take place three times a day. However, mincha (afternoon) and ma'ariv (evening) services are combined.*

long, and a light breakfast is usually served afterward. Although the hour can make it more difficult to organize the early service, in communities where this is common practice, there are groups of "regulars" who can be counted on to make up the *minyan*.

The Torah is read during morning services on Mondays and Thursdays, as well on Shabbat. While Torah reading is not required in a *shiva minyan*, it is permitted, and a scroll may be borrowed from the temple for this purpose. On Shabbat, however, mourners are encouraged to attend services at the synagogue.

Evening services are more typical in the liberal community. These may be held every weeknight of *shiva*, three times, or just once, depending upon the family's wishes. People arrive after dinner (7:30 or 8 P.M.) for the service, which is also about a half hour long.

It is now common practice to take a few minutes during the evening service to invite people to informally share memories of the deceased. This is not a eulogy, though family members and friends may commit their thoughts to paper and read them. Members of the family talk about their loved one or read something of meaning to them, such as a few lines from a *shiva* journal, a poem, or something written by the deceased. The leader of the service can then ask others in the room to share their recollections, too. "That was the high-point of the week for me and my family," said a bereaved son. "My children learned so much about my mother's life from the stories that were told."

This is a good way to involve school-age children, in-laws, and friends, whose mourning often goes unrecognized and who may wish to give voice to their feelings. Even people who didn't know the deceased well, but who care about the bereaved, can add their memories:

"I remember the way your mother beamed whenever her grandchildren walked into the room."

"I didn't know him well, but I met your brother at your wedding, and I remember his big booming laugh."

After hearing the stories, even people who never met the deceased feel connected to his or her memory and can honestly tell mourners, "I wish I'd gotten to know your father. He sounds like a wonderful man."

After evening services, dessert and coffee are served by friends, neighbors, and/or synagogue committee members. While it is inevitable that people will talk about other matters, this is not an ordinary social event and conversation should remain subdued and appropriate. Guests generally leave within an hour or so.

Services can become an organizing principle during a diffuse and difficult week. Said one widow, "If it weren't for the *minyan*, I'm not sure I would have gotten out of bed."

SHABBAT DURING *SHIVA*: Shabbat observance is the core of Jewish practice; more than a holiday, it is an enactment of Judaism's core beliefs about redemption, wholeness, and peace. While Shabbat counts as a full day of *shiva*, the restrictions on public mourning are lifted so as not to dim the joy of the Sabbath. By requiring the bereaved to celebrate Sabbath, Judaism insists that life and hope take precedence over death. "It is forbidden to despair," said Rabbi Nachman of Bratslav. Shabbat is the method that transforms Nachman's statement from a slogan into a way of life.

Some of the visual cues of *shiva* are set aside during the Sabbath. For example, if the memorial candle has been kept in the dining room, it is moved so that the pleasure of the Shabbat candles will be undiminished. Traditionally, mourners also remove the *k'riah* garment or ribbon and are encouraged to attend services at synagogue rather than at home.

Leaving the house for Shabbat services can be a healthy step back into life. At Friday evening services in some temples, mourners enter the sanctuary only after the singing of the hymn *Lecha Dodi*. At that point or later in the service, prior to Kaddish, the rabbi will announce the family's loss. When the time comes for mourners to rise and say Kaddish, they stand among others who have lost a loved one.

You need not belong to a synagogue to attend services at any temple. The rabbi who performed the funeral will certainly welcome you to his or her congregation to say Kaddish, as will family members or friends who are synagogue members.

After services, members of the congregation invariably approach mourners (whether or not they are acquainted) to offer condolences. Mourners stand at a distance from, or leave before, the casual conversation and noshing that takes place at the social gatherings that follow the service: oneg Shabbat (on Friday night) or kiddush (Saturday morning.)

Sometimes, when Shabbat comes early during *shiva*, going out for services can feel disruptive or even disrespectful. And even when the Sabbath falls on the last day of *shiva*, some people are too fragile to accept the kind of attention focused on mourners at a synagogue. For those who are not ready to face a sea of faces, there are private ways to change observance of *shiva* in honor of Shabbat.

For example, if you have not gone outside yet, consider taking a walk. Wear different kinds of clothing (casual if you've been dressed up; dressed up if you've been casual). Sit on the porch rather than in the living room. Put aside the books about bereavement and read something else—perhaps Abraham Joshua Heschel's beautiful little book *The Sabbath*.[8]

SHIVA DURING JEWISH HOLIDAYS: The laws regarding the Jewish holidays' impact on *shiva* are specific and complicated.[9] In general, if mourners have observed *shiva* for any amount of time prior to the holiday, the rest of *shiva* is canceled. If a death occurs on a holiday or during a festival such as Passover, *shiva* begins when the holiday ends.

Canceling or postponing *shiva* on holidays seems counterintuitive to many people. Mourners need to sit with their grief regardless of whether it's Rosh Hashanah or Shavuot. In making these rules, the rabbis weighed the needs of the individual mourner against the community's obligation to celebrate the cycle of the year and decided that the communal needs were paramount—another example of choosing life over death. Since liberal Judaism treats *halachah* as a historical and changing system rather than as divine and immutable law, liberal Jews sometimes choose to continue to sit *shiva* during holidays.

If holiday observance during *shiva* is an issue for you and your family, discuss the subject with your rabbi.

CHILDREN: Parents often keep children away from *shiva*, hoping to protect them from grief. The tradition seems to support this impulse, excusing everyone under the age of thirteen from observing *shiva* or saying Kaddish. However, bereavement experts say that adults sometimes do more harm than good when they try to shield the young. Most rabbis concur and encourage parents to let children visit and/or participate in some part of *shiva*. (See "Children as Mourners" in Chapter 10.)

Children of all ages need extra reassurance in the immediate aftermath of a death. Even babies will be aware of the distress and disruption around them, and preschoolers may worry about their parents dying. *Shiva* can be very reassuring for kids: seeing bereaved parents, grandparents, or friends smile and even laugh as memories surface shows them that the terrible sadness in the air will eventually lift. It also provides a great lesson about how families fit into communities, and how communities can care for families.

Older children may want to participate in services to express their own sorrow and as a way to maintain connections with family members who are preoccupied and distracted. School-aged children can write about their feelings or share pictures they drew.[10] They can also be invited (without any pressure) to share memories of the deceased along with the adults during the time set aside for public reminiscence. Obviously, these options should never be forced upon children, simply offered.

Even so, *shiva* can be very hard on some children, who should be allowed to withdraw if they seem frightened or overwhelmed. Maintaining regular schedules (including school, lessons, and the like) can be helpful; arranging for play dates or even sleepovers away from the *shiva* house may be a good idea.

Most important is that some adult take the time to listen to each child and respond appropriately. When parents are bereaved, they may be unable to bear witness to their children's grief, so another adult—an aunt, uncle, cousin, or friend—should be asked to help.

ENDING *SHIVA*: Since fractions of days count as full days, *shiva* ends in the morning of the seventh day after the funeral. In a traditional home, the week concludes after the mourners say Kaddish at the morning services.

Shiva ends without ritual. However, there are a few customs—some old, some new—that give closure to the week. The best known is the simple practice of the mourners walking around the block together, a symbolic enactment of returning to the world.[11]

But consciously doing anything that you avoided doing during *shiva* can have the same effect. The idea is to make a clear division between time spent in *shiva* and the rest of life. There is one rather dramatic custom of ending the week by hammering a nail into a board.[12] However, even something as simple as putting on leather shoes after a week of wearing slippers will feel strange and new. Men who haven't shaved and women who didn't wear makeup resume their normal habits, facing new selves in undraped mirrors.

Since it is traditional to remove the *k'riah** ribbon or clothing at the end of *shiva,* one mourner created a simple ritual that focuses on mending torn clothing: scarves, neckties, jackets, or sweaters. The family gathers and silently bastes their torn garments, using large, obvious stitches so the tear will still be apparent. When everyone is finished, mourners share their feelings and/or rise and recite the 23rd Psalm.[13]

Although some people are ready and even eager to get back to work after a week of unaccustomed contemplation, some mourners cannot bear the idea of a quick return to "normal." The seventh day can be used for a gentler reentry. Setting aside the to-do list for a few more hours, search out a place where it is pos-

---

* *Some people continue to wear the ribbon after* shiva, *as an outward sign to others that they are still in mourning. See* "Shloshim" *in Chapter 8.*

sible to be "in" the world without yet becoming "of" it. Drive to a park, to the beach, or the mountains. Stroll through an art museum or go to the library. Have lunch with a good friend at a quiet restaurant.

Mourners are not finished grieving when they get up from sitting *shiva*. Nevertheless, it is the end of the beginning. Things change over the course of the first seven days. Grief changes. The bereaved change. The great benefit of *shiva* is that it gives you time to notice the changes.

HOW TO BE A SHIVA VISITOR: Judaism considers comforting the bereaved a sacred obligation. In the words of the great twelfth-century rabbi and physician Maimonides, "The duty of comforting a mourner is greater than the duty of comforting the sick. Why? Because visiting the sick is an act of benevolence upon the living only. Comforting the mourner is an act of benevolence toward both the living and the dead."

Any friend or acquaintance, Jewish or non-Jewish, can call on a bereaved family when they are receiving visitors during *shiva*. This is not a social event: no invitations are issued. According to Jewish law, anyone who learns of a loss in the congregation or neighborhood is both obliged and blessed by the opportunity to perform this *mitzvah*.

Paying a *shiva* visit is never easy, and people are always worried about saying or doing the wrong thing, or of feeling out of place. But the overriding mandate is simply to be there. Showing your face in a house of mourning is, in itself, the most powerful statement of concern, respect, and condolence anyone can make. In the face of death, words are almost beside the point. God instructs the prophet Ezekiel to "sigh in silence"[14] when among mourners.

Many of the normal rules of etiquette are suspended during *shiva*. Mourners live like guests in their own homes: they are served food cooked by others; they let others answer the telephone and door.

The door is usually left unlocked so that mourners will not have to rise to greet people. According to Jewish law, visitors do not even say hello first, but wait to be acknowledged by the bereaved. Visitors follow the social pace set by the mourners. If they are sitting silently, the silence should not be broken. If they are laughing over a happy memory, guests can laugh, too.

In practice, some of these customs are breached—someone rings the doorbell or asks the bereaved how they are doing. There are no dire consequences to such "mistakes," and mourners may be unaware of or unconcerned with these traditions. *Shiva* manners are simply guidelines that stress the importance of treating mourners with the utmost compassion and deference.

There are all kinds of *shiva* visits: formal, intimate, melancholy, sweet. *Shiva* services and announced "visitation" hours convene the whole community around the bereaved, including colleagues from work, neighbors, and acquaintances from temple as well as extended family and close friends. Contact with mourners at such times can be as brief as a hug. These moments are important and precious, but people who want to spend time in more intimate conversation will also visit when the mourner is likely to be alone.

Apart from the times set aside for services, *shiva* tends to be rather informal. People drop by to pay respects, bring food, reminisce, listen, and simply sit with the mourner. Visitors should be sensitive to the mood and energy level of the bereaved. If mourners seem exhausted or are already deep in conversation with someone else, just say a quick hello and ask if you can return at another time. At the end of the week, visits tend to drop off and friends are especially welcome. It may be a good idea to call ahead to schedule a visit.

Consolation is a gentle art that requires flexibility as well as sensitivity. What follows are a few general suggestions for *shiva* visitors:

- *Shiva* visits tend to be brief—usually a half hour to an hour. Visitors approach the mourner, wait for him or her to say hello, and then follow the bereaved's cues. If the mourner wants to talk about her loved one, comforters should stay and listen. However, after a long day of talking, she may be talked out and need to rest.

- If a guest is asked a question about himself, he should answer briefly. This is not a time for long stories about office politics or a grandchild's accomplishments. The conversation should ebb and flow around the deceased, the mourner's emotions, the progress of *shiva*.

- Visitors *should not* try to "cheer up" the mourners. The primary job of the comforter is to listen. In general, it is better to avoid giving advice, presuming to know what the mourner is feeling, or theorizing about how soon he will be "back to normal." It's better to ask questions, share memories, and simply say, "I'm so sorry."

    Nevertheless, visitors in *shiva* houses frequently find themselves remembering their own losses. While it is not appropriate to go into great detail, a statement such as "I lost my wife last year" speaks volumes to the recently bereaved. Mourners are often struck by their new, painfully earned knowledge of the mourning all around them. There is a kind of solidarity among the bereaved: "All go to the house of mourning and each weeps over his own sorrow," wrote Joshua ibn Sahib, a fourteenth-century Spanish biblical scholar.

- It is traditional to bring food to a *shiva* house, but not flowers, candy, liquor, or any other kind of gift. Since friends may already be coordinating meals, it's a good idea to call first to find out what is needed, though many people automatically bring baked goods, which are served to guests throughout the day and after services.

  It is always appropriate to make a charitable donation in honor of the deceased rather bring a gift. If asked, virtually all nonprofit organizations send an acknowledgment to the bereaved family, informing them of your gift. (See "*Tzedakah*" in Chapter 9.)

- Call ahead, especially after the first few days, to offer help in running errands, chauffeuring out-of-town guests, baby-sitting, picking up groceries, etc.

- Say good-bye before you leave.

According to the book of Ecclesiastes, "It is better to go to a house of mourning than to a house of feasting."[15] Of course, most people would rather attend a wedding than a funeral, but paying a *shiva* call can be a profound and beautiful experience. There is an undeniable "rightness" in being there for a friend, colleague, or acquaintance in mourning. Their gratitude is reward enough, but visitors often get more than that. Walking out of a *shiva* house, you savor the air (sweet, cold, heavy, hot), take note of sounds (birds, voices, traffic), breathe deeply, and sigh in gratitude for the gift of being alive.

How to Write a Condolence Card: Like condolence visits, cards and notes are a tangible token of concern and respect. Mourners rarely remember the content of any one sympathy card; however, the fact that it was sent means everything. Perhaps nowhere else does the phrase "It's the thought that counts" ring so true.

There is no need to write at length. Letters that share a personal memory of the deceased are special, but even if she was a stranger to the writer, the simplest message is moving if it comes from the heart:

"I was so sorry to hear . . ."

"I remember when . . ."

"I'm thinking of you."

"I wish you peace."

"I hope you have fond memories to sustain you."

"I love you."

Long-Distance Shiva: The geographic realities of American life mean that many people sit *shiva* far from the comfort of their own homes and communities. Reaching out by phone can help, but there is nothing so consoling as your own friends' understanding faces and hugs, your own rabbi's presence.

It is becoming more and more customary to sit *shiva* in more than one place. For example, after three days in one city, some mourners continue *shiva* at home, either for the rest of the week or just for another day. If the full seven days were observed out of town, mourners sometimes have a *shiva*-like memorial commemoration in their own homes when they return.

Your rabbi or cantor may lead the service or say a few words at the gathering. If the week of *shiva* is formally over, mourners can invite friends over to share memories of the loved one and say

Kaddish together. Contrary to many mourners' fears, bringing *shiva* back home is not an imposition on others. As sad as it is, comforting one's friend is a very meaningful *mitzvah*.

For mourners who are uncomfortable with the idea of extending *shiva* or just too exhausted to be with a group of people immediately following their return home, a memorial observance at the end of the *shloshim*, the first month, is an option. (See Chapter 8.)

"NO VISITATION": When these words appear at the end of a death notice or in the rabbi's remarks at the funeral, a family announces its decision to forgo the comforts as well as the rigors of *shiva*.

There are many reasons why people decide against *shiva*. If someone dies after a long illness and months or even years of anticipatory grieving, the family may feel that *shiva* is superfluous. People who are not affiliated with a synagogue or any other Jewish organization and have only a small circle of friends may fear being isolated during *shiva*. Overscheduled people feel the pressure of their many responsibilities: children, colleagues, deadlines, bills.

Some people view *shiva* as morbid and counterintuitive. Death unlocks all kinds of painful emotional floodgates, and human beings, like all living creatures, seek to avoid suffering rather than wait for the next exhausting spasm of tears. And *shiva* raises profound questions about belief, identity, affiliation. For people whose connection to Judaism is passive or ambivalent, being part of such a traditional Jewish ritual may seem contrived or hypocritical or simply uncomfortable. "No visitation" bypasses consideration of such issues.

But "no visitation" announcements are becoming rarer. Those

who sit with their grief during *shiva*—sometimes reinterpreting laws and customs, sometimes inventing new traditions—discover that the ritual is a precious and healing gift.[16]

Whatever your decisions about sitting *shiva*—where, how long, how to, or even whether—the seven days that follow the funeral of a loved one are bound to be highly charged. It will be: The First Monday Since He Died. The First Friday Since She Died. At its core, *shiva* is the way that Jewish mourners begin to tell time after a loved one dies.

CHAPTER EIGHT

THE FIRST YEAR

THE YEAR AFTER A LOSS IS FILLED WITH LESSONS NO ONE wants to learn: how to watch the trees turn red and gold without her; how to lead a seder alone; how to smile at a bar mitzvah that would have been the light of his life. The work of grief over the course of the first year is about relearning how to live in the world. And it's hard.

Jewish law and custom acknowledge the changes of the first year in many ways. According to tradition, mourners change their accustomed seats in the synagogue—a literal shift both in personal perspective and within the community. Saying Kaddish formalizes daily and/or weekly remembrance. Holidays (including Shabbat) are milestones through the journey. Rituals end the first month (*shloshim*) and the first year (*shanah*) in ways that create closure and affirm continuity.

Judaism's "architecture of time" for mourners continues even after the first year with the saying of Kaddish in the annual commemorations of *yahrzeit* and Yizkor. But the first year is a year of unwelcome firsts.

Liberal Jews observe the customs and rituals that are described in this section in a variety of ways. Some people add new observances, such as planting a tree at the close of *shloshim;* some transform old customs and, for example, say Kaddish as a private meditation. Some find wisdom, comfort, and strength in following traditions abandoned by parents or even grandparents, such as attending daily services in order to say Kaddish. Making these choices is part of grieving and healing, too.

SHLOSHIM: THE FIRST MONTH

Jewish law obligates official mourners (children, spouses, siblings, and parents) to continue with some of the observances of *shiva* for thirty days after the funeral, a period that includes the week of *shiva.*

During *shloshim*—the word means "thirty"—mourners return to work and regular family responsibilities, but tradition maintains a "fence" that permits grieving to continue. The prohibitions of *shloshim,* which are mostly concerned with public obligations, protect mourners against rushing or being rushed through their sorrow. In a culture that expects people to "get on with it" after a few days, *shloshim* helps the individual and the community to be patient and mindful that grief cannot and should not be hurried.

During *shloshim,* distractions and everyday pleasures are limited. Traditionally, the bereaved don't listen to music or attend concerts, plays, movies, or sporting events. People don't wear new clothing and men forgo haircuts and even shaving. Liberal Jews interpret these restrictions in ways that are personally meaningful: for example, some people avoid watching any television or listening to music on the radio; others limit themselves to news and public affairs programs.

Mourners avoid most social gatherings. Although someone observing *shloshim* would probably attend a family wedding or bar mitzvah, she might leave before the *simcha,* or reception. Although there is no Jewish law against it, mourners do not visit the cemetery during the first month. While this notion may have been born of superstition—it was thought that the spirit lingered on earth for a period of time after burial—it also keeps the bereaved in the world of the living. In the words of the *Shulchan Aruch,* "One must not grieve excessively for the dead."[1]

Shloshim is not a period of self-deprivation, however. Mourners resume many private pleasures, such as reading and study, visiting friends, exercise, playing with children. In many circumstances, mourners are permitted to marry during the thirty days.[2] Sexual relations are permitted. The bereaved are required to get out of the house to attend services and say Kaddish. The requirements of *shloshim* may be terminated by the observance of Rosh Hashanah, Yom Kippur, Sukkot, Passover, and Shavuot. (Mourning observance during holidays is best discussed with your rabbi.)

Life resumes its precedence over death, but mourners keep their distance from the full court press of daily life. Some people even wear a *k'riah* ribbon or torn garment for a full month. Although tradition dictates that it be removed at the end of *shiva,* the ribbon is a silent announcement of the mourner's emotional state during the first month, signaling colleagues, friends, and acquaintances that its wearer is still fragile and not yet entirely "of" the workday world.

The ribbon also alerts people who might not know of a loss to offer condolences and, if they have experienced bereavement themselves, empathize. Mourners are often amazed at the discovery of loss around them. In the words of the great medieval rabbi known as Rashi, "Bereavement is like a wheel encircling the world."[3]

Another way to acknowledge the first month is by reconvening the principal mourners around a table for a Friday evening Shabbat meal or by attending Friday night or Saturday morning services. The weekly cycle can provide a structure for reflection, such as writing in a journal just before lighting Shabbat candles, or composing a "letter" to the deceased to record thoughts, conversations, and changes that occurred since the last Friday night. Attending Shabbat services marks the passing of the month within the comfort and context of a larger community.

Shloshim can be an extremely busy time. Some mourners feel compelled to "take care of business" as soon as possible, clearing out the now-vacant house, disposing of property, meeting with lawyers, changing documents, and the like. Many people spend hours writing thank-you notes in response to sympathy cards, donations made in memory of the deceased, and *shiva* calls. (Funeral homes sell personalized thank-you notes for this purpose.)

However, some mourners are too exhausted or numb to do much of anything for the first thirty days, and for them *shloshim* is a "lost" month. As the reality of death sinks in, the overwhelming sorrow of *shiva* may return at any time. Friends tend to remain quite solicitous during *shloshim*, checking in on the mourner, inviting her out for meals. Nevertheless, the formal daily support of *shiva* may be gone. Widows and widowers spend their first nights alone. The days grow emptier. New symptoms related to grief may surface; for example, sleep disturbances are very common.

SAYING KADDISH: The primary ritual obligation for mourners during *shloshim* is saying Kaddish in memory of the deceased. According to Jewish law, Kaddish is recited aloud only in the presence of a *minyan* of ten adult Jews, which means the mourner must seek out a community in which to pray.[4] (See Part I, "Why We Say Kaddish.")

Liberal Jews make all kinds of choices about saying Kaddish in memory of a loved one. Some people attend two services daily, others go once a day, and many say Kaddish once a week at Shabbat services.

Daily synagogue services are held morning and/or evening, depending on the individual temple. All Orthodox and some Conservative synagogues have two daily *minyans*. Some Conservative, Reform, and Reconstructionist temples hold one daily service, morning or evening, but many do not. If you with to say Kaddish daily but belong to a synagogue that has no daily *minyan*, your rabbi can direct you to a congregation that does.

Everyone is welcome at synagogue services, and mourners generally find a warm embrace wherever they go for Kaddish. If you are not a temple member, shop around for a comfortable place. Attend services at the congregations in your neighborhood or near your workplace. Seek recommendations from the rabbi who officiated at the funeral, the funeral home director, family members, and friends.

For many mourners, attending services to say Kaddish becomes the organizing principle for their grief, a time for reflection, and a way to connect. People who attend a daily *minyan* in order to say Kaddish find themselves among other mourners who quickly become an empathic community. Those who were not previously synagogue regulars may find this a transforming experience: an introductory and/or refresher course in Hebrew and Jewish worship, an inspiration to continue studying, and a doorway into the Jewish world.[5] Mourners sometimes form close friendships and join the congregations where they say Kaddish.

One woman explains, "At the time of my loss, the *minyan* introduced a whole new set of people to my life, people I quickly came to care about. I wondered how their vacations or operations went and where they were if they missed a morning or evening. . . . Kaddish is a bond between generations, but the bonds among mourners who share the Kaddish experience may be equally powerful."[6]

Less traditionally, some mourners use Kaddish as a daily personal prayer. "It was my private meditation for that month," said a man who recited Kaddish every morning for his sister. "I'm not much of a synagogue-goer, but the sound of that prayer means something to me. It's my time of day to think, cry, sigh, whatever."

ENDING *SHLOSHIM*: The thirty days are the full measure of mourning for spouses, parents, and siblings. Only children are required to observe the rituals of *shanah*, the first year, though other mourners often do.

There are several ways to mark the end of *shloshim*. A family can invite friends and members of their community to join them for an evening *minyan*, study session, or simply for a gathering to reminisce. This can be especially consoling if *shiva* took place out of town.

People who have been wearing a *k'riah* ribbon or garment usually remove it at the end of *shloshim*. This can be done simply and without ceremony or it can become the occasion for an intimate ritual like the one described in Chapter 7. Similarly, family and close friends can gather for a quiet meal, light a memorial candle, and share their experiences of the past month. And as with virtually all Jewish milestones, the end of *shloshim* can be an occasion for making a charitable contribution in memory of the person who died.

A nice way to conclude *shloshim* is by planting a tree in memory of the loved one. Reverence for trees is a recurrent theme in Jewish texts, and the Torah itself is called "a tree of life." Memorial contributions in support of reforestation programs in Israel may be sent to the Jewish National Fund.* A hands-on tree planting is a more tangible symbol of continuity.

Family members and close friends might gather in a backyard, at a local park, or on the grounds of a synagogue or Jewish community center (with permission, of course). People can take turns covering the roots with soil, watering, and telling stories of the deceased. Although the shovel may well recall the pain of filling in the grave only thirty days earlier, the act of planting is a way of bringing memory to life.[7] Some people find the symbolism of a fruit or flowering tree especially beautiful.

SHANAH: A YEAR'S TIME

Jewish tradition is quite firm about time limits on outward signs of grief. According to the *Shulchan Aruch*, "Whoever weeps more than the law requires must be weeping for something else. Rather, let one accept the schedule set down by the sages: three days for weeping, seven for lamenting, 30 days for mourning."[8]

Even so, Jewish practice acknowledges that mourners suffer for longer than a month and indeed mandates a special yearlong status for the bereaved. "Whoever sees a mourner within 30 days should comfort him but not ask him how he is feeling. After 30 days but within 12 months, he should ask how he is and then comfort him."[9]

For most mourners, public signs of grief end with *shloshim*.

---

* *Call 800-542-TREE.*

However, according to tradition, children continue saying Kaddish and observing some of the same prohibitions on public rejoicing as during the first thirty days. The year of mourning is counted from the day of death, and traditionally consists of either eleven or twelve months according to the lunar Hebrew, or Jewish, calendar, though some liberal Jews count the year of mourning using the Gregorian, or secular, calendar.[10]

The longer period for children is often explained by citing the sixth commandment: "Honor your father and your mother."[11] But to many, this seems counterintuitive; after all, parents are "supposed to" die before children. Parents who bury a child and bereaved spouses would seem in greater need of rituals to give shape to their grief.

But this ruling, like so many others, dates from times when human lives were shorter and when infant and child mortality touched every family. In those days, limiting requirements for public mourning was doubtlessly intended to keep people from focusing on their losses to the exclusion of other obligations—such as remarrying and having more children.

Despite the fact that bereaved parents, spouses, and siblings are not required to continue public mourning, there is no prohibition against it. Indeed, many "exempt" mourners say Kaddish for their loved one for the full year, and it is common to find as many widows and widowers as bereaved sons and daughters at a daily *minyan*. Bereaved life partners, siblings, grandchildren, parents, and close friends may choose to mourn for the full year, too.

During the year of mourning, many of the prohibitions of *shloshim* continue. Mourners avoid parties and other purely social gatherings, though attendance at family events, such as weddings and bar and bat mitzvahs, is permitted. Tradition prohibits listening to instrumental music, or attending plays and concerts. Liberal Jews tend to view such restrictions as a matter of personal choice.

As with other phases of Jewish mourning, there are positive *mitzvot* as well as negative ones during *shana*. The positive commandments for the year of mourning include prayer, study, and *tzedakah*—three interconnected blessings.

PRAYER: Kaddish continues as in *shloshim*. Mourners who attend services on a regular basis—whether once or twice daily, a few times a week, or weekly on Shabbat—find it works as a polestar through a difficult time. Mourners often form a community of their own, reaching out to people with new losses, healing themselves by helping others through the darkest days of grief.

As the year progresses and daily life gathers momentum, mourners sometimes feel guilty for "forgetting" their loved one for an hour or even a day at a time. Saying Kaddish regularly is a way of both giving grief standing and of containing it. As one woman wrote, "I think about my mother while I say Kaddish. Knowing that I have a structured way of remembering and that I'll be coming back to her memory again in the evening frees me to go about the rest of my day unburdened. Of course, I think of my mother during the day as well, but it isn't painful."[12]

There are two traditions about counting the year of saying Kaddish. The Talmud prescribes a full twelve months. However, in the sixteenth century, the legal scholar Rabbi Moses Isserles[13] shortened the period to eleven months based on the belief that only totally evil souls stood before God's judgment for a full year. Since no son or daughter should consider their parent completely wicked, this abbreviation was seen as an act of respect.

Stopping after eleven months also speaks to the psychological needs of the mourner, which intensify during the four weeks leading up to the anniversary of the death. During the twelfth month, mourners may be overwhelmed by memories of the final illness and/or death; they may also be preoccupied with preparations for the upcoming *yahrzeit* and an unveiling of the grave marker. Saying Kaddish in addition to all of this may mean devoting too much time to death.[14]

However, when the obligation to say Kaddish as a mourner does come to an end, some people experience the transition as a loss of purpose, community, and connection to the deceased:

> This first year was about showing up, a place to go, a community of words that were his words. For this year he has been nearby, alive in these words he learned by heart as a boy. . . .
>
> It has been soothing to stand here, understanding him more fully as his values wash over me. Now he is going even farther away. I am an orphan now—an orphan who is no longer a Kaddish. Where do I find him? Where do I find myself?[15]

Of course, there is no reason to stop attending daily prayers if the experience has become a source of comfort, connection, and identity. After all, it is a *mitzvah* to pray daily, and those who attend services help provide a *minyan* so that others can say Kaddish.

STUDY: Undertaking a new aspect of Jewish learning is considered an eloquent tribute to the life of the deceased. Attending services regularly to say Kaddish can be a learning experience in itself. Mourners become familiar with the order of the service and improve their Hebrew skills, almost without trying. One traditional study goal is to learn to lead some or all of the daily service—an honor offered to people on the last day they say Kaddish as official mourners. Family members and close friends can be invited for this occasion—a unique living tribute to the memory of a loved one.

Whether or not they lead services, people who have been "regulars" sometimes sponsor a Kiddush breakfast for the morning *minyan* on their last day as official mourners. Not exactly a celebration, the meal commemorates a milestone in the mourner's grief.

There are other forms of study besides learning the service. Some mourners attend Torah study sessions (held before Shabbat morning services in many congregations) to honor the memory of a loved one. Others devote time to learning Hebrew or Jewish history or the rituals of the life cycle.

TZEDAKAH: The tradition of giving *tzedakah* to honor a personal milestone becomes poignant, urgent, and ultimately triumphant after a death. Giving money to charity is one way of keeping the memory of a loved one alive and palpable in the world. During the first year, some mourners make contributions in memory of a loved one at regular intervals; for instance, every time they say Kaddish, which is why there are *pushkes*, or little alms boxes, set out at synagogue minyans. Study and *tzedakah* merge when mourners sponsor a lecture or scholarship in memory of a loved one. (See Chapter 9.)

SEASON TO SEASON: From the end of *shloshim* until the anniversary of a death, mourners endure a series of heartbreaking "firsts." The annual cycle of Jewish holidays may seem especially empty and difficult if Rosh Hashanah was always associated with a big dinner at Nana's, or if Hanukkah was Pop's favorite.

These milestones in the Jewish calendar often prompt a return of intense feelings of grief and loss, which is perfectly normal. But the calendar also provides four occasions for mourners to publicly acknowledge their losses during the Yizkor prayer, which is recited at a service which is also called Yizkor—a word that means "memorial." Yizkor is held on Yom Kippur and at the end of the three "pilgrimage" festivals: Sukkot,[16] Passover, and Shavuot. (See Chapter 9.)

For some reason, joyful family celebrations seem to proliferate in the wake of a death. The absence of the deceased seems cruel when a new baby is born, a grandson gets married, a daughter becomes bat mitzvah. But even these events can provide opportunities to remember the departed and to make their presence felt. At baby namings and *brisses,* during wedding toasts and bar or bat mitzvah banquets, there is always an appropriate moment to recall the names and faces of people who are missing and who are missed.

Recalling loved ones during happy occasions adds a bittersweet note, but ultimately it is the sweetness that lingers. Speaking about someone who would have so loved the events of the day brings the continuity of generations into plain sight. After a recent loss, giving voice to the sadness in many hearts also gives permission for family and friends to comfort one another.

As the months pass, mourners find themselves more and more alone with their grief. Friends stop calling or dropping by as often. Acquaintances and colleagues start treating mourners as though they had returned to "normal."

The bereaved sometimes feel like they are falling apart precisely when they think they should be "getting better." This is not cause for undue alarm. Bereavement experts note that grief pays "visits," which are better off welcomed than avoided or ignored. Nevertheless, the isolation of grief does sometimes lead to serious depression. As difficult as it may be, mourners need to stay connected to others.

YAHRZEIT

Grief can become intense and even overwhelming as the first year comes to an end. Indeed, the "anniversary reaction" can extend to a whole season; if the death occurred in the springtime, the appearance of crocuses may be forever tinged with sadness.

As the anniversary of a death approaches, mourners often revisit the last days of a loved one's life, remembering the details of the same month of the previous year:

Today was the day . . .

   . . . I got the phone call.
   . . . he went into the hospital.
   . . . she lapsed into a coma.
   . . . we gathered at the bedside and said good-bye.

Jews call the anniversary of a death *yahrzeit*, Yiddish for "a year's time." The observance of this milestone is both private and public, intimate and communal.

THE DATE: The annual remembrance is traditionally marked according to the Hebrew calendar; if a loved one died on the eighth day in the month of Av, the *yahrzeit* falls on the eighth of Av in all subsequent years. Since the lunar year does not correspond to the secular calendar, Hebrew dates "jump around" on the secular calendar: so the eighth of Av may fall on August 4 one year and August 15 the following year. This presents no difficulty for anyone who owns a Jewish calendar, which is laid out according to the secular year but also lists Hebrew dates.[17] Jewish funeral homes send out calendars to anyone who has used their services, and also mail annual reminders of *yahrzeit* dates to principal mourners. Many synagogues send *yahrzeit* reminders to their members.

Some liberal Jews find it more emotionally meaningful (as well as easier to remember) to observe the *yahrzeit* as the day of death on the secular calendar. This fulfills, too, the religious purpose of *yahrzeit*—which is to honor the memory of a loved one.

PRIVATE OBSERVANCES: The best-known *yahrzeit* is lighting a twenty-four-hour memorial candle. The small, flickering light—a universal symbol of the soul—is both melancholy and consoling. It gives form to memory: visible, warm, incandescent.

Since Jewish days begin at sunset, the candle is lit on the evening before the day of death. There is no set time; before or after sunset is fine, except on Shabbat or the evening before a holiday, when the *yahrzeit* candle is lit prior to lighting Shabbat and/or festival candles.

Yahrzeit candles are available in Judaica shops, kosher grocery stores, and supermarkets that serve Jewish customers. The candles are white and set inside a small, transparent glass. Many people have memories of these little glasses from childhood, when grandparents recycled them into drinking glasses.

There is no *b'racha,* no fixed blessing for lighting a *yahrzeit* candle. Many people recite a private personal prayer, sometimes beginning or ending with the phrase,

זִכְרוֹנוֹ/זִכְרוֹנָהּ לִבְרָכָה:

Zichrono/Zichronah livrachah

May his/her memory be a blessing.[18]

The candle may be placed anywhere in the home, and is usually are permitted to burn all the way down. Sometimes, family members surround the light with photographs of the deceased, a much-loved book, children's pictures, or letters. This can remind children of a grandparent they may not remember well, or introduce them to someone they never met.

Some people use candle-lighting as a focus for memory, an occasion for leafing through photo albums, watching videos of the deceased, listening to his or her favorite music, adding another entry to a grief journal. Family members and close friends sometimes gather and take turns sharing a memory of the deceased, and/or reading a poem or prayer. Every member of a family may light their own candle, a token of their unique relationship and loss.

In addition to lighting a candle, mourners might reread a journal written in the immediate aftermath of the death, look at the *shiva* guest book and condolence cards, or listen to music unheard for the past twelve months.

Some people pay a *yahrzeit* visit to the grave, to recite psalms and the *El Malei Rachamim* prayer. It is also considered a *mitzvah* to study from Jewish texts at the graveside. (See Chapter 9 for more about visiting the grave.)

PUBLIC OBSERVANCES: *Yahrzeit* also provides communal consolation for the predictable pangs of sorrow that return on the anniversary of death. In the synagogue, every *yahrzeit* has a weeklong presence. Starting on the Shabbat before the anniversary, the names of temple members' loved ones may be recited during services. In congregations with memorial plaques on their walls, an electric light may be lit beside the names as well. In some temples, the weekly newsletter lists those for whom Kaddish is being recited.

Saying the Mourner's Kaddish in a *minyan* is the central element of public mourning at a *yahrzeit*. Liberal Jews do this in several different ways. Some people say their *yahrzeit* Kaddish at the Shabbat services immediately prior to the anniversary of death; others make a point of attending services on the day itself. In some congregations, people observing a *yahrzeit* are called to the Torah for an *aliyah*. At most daily *minyans,* only mourners or those observing *yahrzeits* stand during the Mourner's Kaddish. With the bereaved thus identified, people invariably approach after services to offer a few words of condolence and a hug.

As at every meaningful juncture in Jewish life, it is traditional to give money to a charity on the occasion of a *yahrzeit*. Synagogues that send out *yahrzeit* reminders usually include an envelope for contributions.

....

CHAPTER NINE

THE CONSOLATIONS
OF MEMORY

You are remembered in love.
You are part of the now in me.
  All the good,
  All the love,
All the comfort a person can give
Is remembered
  And repeated
  For your sake.
Time changes,
Everything passes,
  But love.
Peace abide you.[1]

GERALD DICKER

As TIME PASSES and grief changes, memory can become a
teacher, an inspiration, a cherished companion. Memory can

become a source of meaning and a catalyst for good in the world. In other words, a blessing.

זִכְרוֹנוֹ/זִכְרוֹנָהּ לִבְרָכָה:

Zichrono/Zichronah livrachah

May his/her memory be a blessing.

Memory is given shape among Jews in many ways, some as tangible as a granite headstone. Some are liturgical, as in the periodic Yizkor service; others are as practical and public as a building named in honor of a loved one. And some are as incandescent as a baby's name.

AT THE CEMETERY

A traditional Hebrew expression of consolation is *Ha-makom yenahem otcha/otach*—May God comfort you. The word *Ha-makom* has a double meaning: not only is it one of God's names; it also means "the place." So the phrase can be translated "May this place comfort you."

GRAVESTONES: The grave, a person's *bet ha-olam*, or eternal home, is where memory takes a solid form. The Hebrew word for a grave marker is *matzevah*, whose root means "to guard" or "bear witness." In the Bible, *matzevot* were erected to commemorate formal agreements and to memorialize moments of great awe, as well as to mark graves, as when Jacob gathered rocks to mark the place he buried Rachel, his wife.[2]

While there has never been a standard shape or size for headstones, Jewish tradition frowned upon elaborate graves, citing pagan and especially Egyptian excess in burying the dead.[3] Jewish cemeteries tend to follow the ancient preference for simplicity.[4]

Of course, it is impossible to completely ignore social pressures to "do right by" the dead. Thus, Jewish gravestones through the ages have varied in response to local customs and fashions. Today, their sizes and shapes are largely dictated by the rules and regulations of the cemetery in which they are erected, which vary widely. At one end of the spectrum are the old, crowded "cities" of tombstones with a variety of headstones. By contrast, the newer "memorial parks" are wide-open spaces, dotted by unobtrusive and uniform markers, which lie flat on the ground. (See pp. 64–66 for more about Jewish cemeteries.)

While most people believe that mourners must wait for a year before erecting the tombstone, Jewish law actually permits the monument to go up any time after *shiva* ends; indeed, promptness is seen as an act of respect. Even people who are sitting *shiva* may begin making plans for the stone. In practice, however, mourners rarely make arrangements until the second half of the year, usually in anticipation of the anniversary of a death and a ceremonial unveiling of the headstone.

Gravestones can cost anywhere from several hundred to many thousands of dollars, depending on size and the amount and complexity of lettering and other carving. People tend to select monument companies based on recommendations from friends, rabbis, funeral directors, and cemetery personnel. Memorial parks usually sell their own flat markers. Obviously, Jewish monument makers are most experienced at Hebrew lettering and symbols; however, expert non-Jewish stonecutters do excellent work as well, especially now that computers can provide exact templates.

Prior to meeting with a monument maker, make sure you know the cemetery's rules about size, shape, and design. Jewish cemeteries usually prohibit images of animals and some do not permit any representations of the deceased either. Have the exact location of the grave in hand as well as the deceased's Hebrew name and dates. Call the stonecutter to ask if any other information is needed.

Sometimes, the deceased will have left clear instructions about the headstone; some people even order and pay for their own monuments to spare their heirs the cost. In cases where one spouse died earlier and a double headstone was erected, mourners will simply arrange for the addition of name and date to the stone.

Simplicity is typical of Jewish tombstones, and many display little more than names and dates. However, local customs find their way into Jewish cemeteries, so in America, lines of poetry and terms of endearment are also common.

Name and date are usually engraved in both English and Hebrew. The Ashkenazic custom for tombstones names the father; for example, *Shimon ben Avraham*—Simon son of Abraham. Sephardic tradition names the mother: *Shimon ben Leah*—Simon son of Leah. Or both parents' names may be included: *Shimon ben Avraham v' Leah*, Simon son of Abraham and Leah.

Two sets of dates—birth and death—are usually engraved, one according to the Hebrew calendar, the other using secular dates. In some communities, only the Hebrew date of death is carved.

Apart from names and dates, everything else that appears on

a Jewish headstone is a matter of local custom and personal taste. Many people include important relationships, so words such as "mother and grandmother" or "father and teacher" often appear. The same goes for words of endearment such as "beloved." Sometimes a line from Psalms or part of a favorite poem are engraved as well.

Many Jewish monuments have some Hebrew letters at the top or in an upper corner of the stone. Ashkenazic stones often include the letters פ׳ נ, Pei and Nun, acronym for *poh nikbar*, "here is buried." In Sephardic cemeteries, the letters מ׳ ק, Mem and Kuf, appear, shorthand for *matzevet k'vurat*, "the tombstone of . . ." or *makom kevurah*, "place of burial."

Another traditional Hebrew acronym that appears on many stones is ת׳ נ׳ צ׳ ב׳ ה, Tav, Nun, Tzadi, Bet, and Hey, the first letters of the phrase *t'hey nafsho(ah) tzerurah bitzror ha-hayyim*, which means "May his/her soul be bound up in the bonds of eternal life."

Ornamentation on Jewish headstones tends to be simple. The most common symbol is the six-pointed Magen David, or Star of David. Jews who count themselves as descended from *kohanim*—the priestly caste of the ancient Temple—sometimes include a pair of hands with fingers spread in a chevronlike pose, which some rabbis still use when delivering the priestly benediction. Similarly, Levites may engrave a symbol of the vessel used in ritual hand-washing. East European and Russian Jews sometimes affix engraved cameos of the deceased to the stone.

UNVEILINGS: In many parts of the Jewish world, gravestones are erected within a month of burial without any special ceremony. But among American Jews, it is customary to have a ritual unveiling of the stone on or near the first anniversary of the death.[5]

Unveilings are melancholy and often tearful services where prayers are recited and memories of the deceased are shared. They are not second funerals, however, and are attended by immediate family and a few close friends only. (Some people do send out "unveiling cards," which should always include a detailed map showing the precise location of the grave.)

There are no rules for unveilings, and customs vary. The headstone may be covered by a cloth, though sometimes it is not. Rabbis and cantors may be present to read psalms and lead mourners through the memorial prayer and Kaddish, though there is no liturgical or *halachic* reason for them to attend, nor are they always able to.

Although all rabbinic manuals contain a short service for unveilings, the liturgy is not fixed. A congregational lay leader or family member can lead the service, which generally contains a psalm or two, the memorial prayer (*El Malei Rachamim*), and a recitation of Kaddish. But the "scripted" elements of any unveiling ceremony should be thought of as a kind of ritual platform for sharing personal memories of the deceased.

AN UNVEILING CEREMONY*

To everything there is a season;
A time for everything under the sun.
A time to be born and a time to die,
A time to laugh and a time to mourn,
A time to seek and a time to lose.

This is a time we gather to remember
   someone who gave meaning to our lives.
This is the time we recall
   the bonds that hold us, the love we shared
   the memories that sustain us.[6]

PSALM 121

I will lift up my eyes unto the mountains.
What is the source of my help?
My help comes from Adonai,
Maker of heaven and earth.

Ever watchful, You guide my steps
Guardian of Israel, You never slumber or sleep.
Always near us, You protect us
In daylight and moonlight

   * *A ceremony like this may be led by a cantor or rabbi, or*
   readings may be shared among those gathered at the grave.

You are our strength against evil
Guarding our lives
You watch over our going and coming
From moment to moment, beyond forever

WE ARE LOVED . . .

We are loved by an unending love.
We are embraced by arms that find us
even when we are hidden from ourselves.
We are touched by fingers that soothe us
even when we are too proud for soothing.
We are counseled by voices that guide us
even when we are too embittered to hear.
We are loved by an unending love.
We are supported by hands that uplift us
even in the midst of a fall.
We are urged on by eyes that meet us
even when we are too weak for meeting.
We are loved by an unending love.
Embraced, touched, soothed, and counseled,
Ours are the arms, the fingers, the voices;
Ours are the hands, the eyes, the smiles;
We are loved by an unending love.

RABBI RAMI M. SHAPIRO[7]

(If the stone is covered, the cloth is removed.)

In memory of _____ we establish and consecrate this monument. It is a token of our deep love and respect. You are remembered now, and forever, part of the good in each of us.

May his/her soul be bound up in the bonds of life.

Memories are shared.

PSALM 23

Adonai is my shepherd,
I shall not want.
You cradle me in green pastures,
You lead me beside still waters;
You restore my soul.
You guide me in the paths of righteousness,
For you are righteous.
Yea, though I walk through the valley of the shadow
    of death,
I will fear no evil.
For You are with me.
Your rod and your staff comfort me.
Surely goodness and mercy will follow me
    all the days of my life,
And I will dwell in the house of the Lord, forever.

El Malei Rachamim is sung.*

The Mourner's Kaddish is recited.†

(As they leave, mourners place pebbles atop the headstone, and/or drop torn blades of grass on the grave—customs explained below.)

* *See p. 79.*
† *See pp. 202–212 for translations of and poems based on Kaddish.*

VISITING THE GRAVE: Although it is considered proper and an act of respect to visit the cemetery occasionally, Jewish law discourages mourners from too-frequent trips. Mourning more than required is viewed as a transgression against life.[8] Thus, visits are not permitted on Shabbat, Passover, Sukkot, and Purim, to prevent mourning on what are meant to be joyful days.[9] Jews of Ashkenazic origin, which includes most American Jews, do not visit the grave until at least thirty days after burial. Sephardic Jews go soon after *shiva*.[10]

Traditionally, people visit graves every *yahrzeit* and in the weeks before the high holidays. Some visit on birthdays or wedding anniversaries, or other days that hold personal significance. Synagogues and cemeteries sometimes hold graveside memorial services in the weeks before Rosh Hashanah.

A loved one's grave can be a good place for reflection as well as comfort. If a bride or groom has lost a parent, a prewedding visit to the cemetery can be healing and cathartic. There is sadness and sometimes guilt at moments of great joy when survivors think, "If only she had lived long enough to be here for this day."

Some Jews pray at the graveside; the tradition suggests Psalms and the memorial *El Malei Rachamim* and studying the Talmud. Most people who pray, however, simply pray from their hearts.

The rabbis of old were alarmed at the prospect of Jews praying *to* the dead, an act that seemed pagan and even idolatrous to them. Nevertheless, speaking to one's dead can be a part of grief work. Rabbi Jack Riemer, who has written extensively about bereavement, says, "You've got to forgive the dead and you've got to get forgiveness from the dead and your life is not complete until you do. . . . If you didn't work it out while they were alive, then you try to work it out after they're dead. . . . that's what cemetery visits do."[11]

Apart from showing respect (no eating, loud voices, no walking over graves if at all possible) there are few rules about visiting the grave. Mourners go to sit and be quiet, to reflect, cry, and remember. Some tidy the area. Many drop torn blades of grass on it, recalling the psalmist's image, "Man, his days are like those of grass."[12]

Generally, Jews do not leave flowers at the grave; they leave pebbles instead.

This custom of leaving stones rather than flowers may date back to biblical times. When a *matzevah* was no more than a pile of stones, adding another rock may have been a way to maintain and keep the grave clearly marked. Later, Jewish law explicitly prohibited flowers, which smacked of pagan practices to the rabbis of the Talmud. Like a flower, a pebble is a sign of love and remembrance. But unlike flowers, which wither, stones persist.

Stones turn out to be eloquent graveside mementos; substantial as loss, heavy as grief, enduring as memory.[13]

YIZKOR

On Yom Kippur, when more Jews attend services than on any other day of the year, sanctuaries are at their fullest during the Yizkor service. Yizkor is the name of both a specific prayer and the service during which it is recited. The word means "memorial" and is based on the three-letter Hebrew root *zayin, kaf, raysh: zachor*—remember.

Although there are four Yizkor services throughout the year, it is on Yom Kippur, the most solemn and self-reflective day of the year, that the community as a whole joins together in remembrance of its loved ones—those who died in the year just passing and those who died long ago. Yizkor names the grief of parents, children, spouses, and siblings. It recognizes the loss of cousins and aunts, friends and teachers. Ever since the Holocaust, Yizkor recalls the victims of Nazi Germany.

Every High Holy Day prayer book, or *machzor*, includes several paragraphs dedicated to the memory, respectively, of mother, father, brother, sister, son, daughter, husband, and wife. In addition to these eight, there are also Yizkor prayers for other relatives, friends, martyrs, victims of the Holocaust, and for all the Jewish dead. Mourners can choose to pray one for each of their dead, or read one prayer for all of them. These are read silently, in Hebrew or English.

> May God remember the soul of those who have gone to eternal rest. In loving memory of their lives, I pledge charity to help perpetuate the ideals that were important to them.
>
> Through such deeds and through prayer and memory, their souls are bound up in the bonds of life. May I prove myself worthy of the gift of life and the many other gifts with which they blessed me. May their memory be forever a blessing.

During the brief service, there may be a reading of the names of congregants and/or family members of congregants who have died within the past year, or all of the dead for whom members of the congregation say Kaddish. The custom in some temples is not to read the names, but publish them in a Yizkor book.

Before the service ends, the cantor chants the *El Malei Rachamim* and a heartfelt Kaddish is recited.

According to Jewish law, mourners may say the Yizkor prayer by themselves; unlike Kaddish, there is no requirement for a *minyan*. Nevertheless, this is a prayer that, although read silently by each person, gains power from the fact that mourners stand shoulder-to-shoulder. The sanctuary fills with the sounds of sighs and tears. One rabbi calls Yizkor a "ritual embodiment of our unending conversation with the dead."[14]

There are many customs about who should and who should not attend Yizkor services. In some congregations, people whose parents are both alive take care to be out of the sanctuary during Yizkor, based on a superstition that they might "cause" a death by being there. This is a folk belief of such long standing, that even people who dismiss it still leave before the service begins, either out of habit or to honor the custom. Many congregations encourage parents not to bring young children to Yizkor, to preserve the mood and focus of the service. Mourners can attend Yizkor services during the first year after a death; there is no need to wait until after the *yahrzeit*, although that is customary in many congregations.[15]

The Yizkor service is a relatively recent addition to Jewish practice. It became part of the Yom Kippur liturgy as a memorial to those murdered during the Crusades of the twelfth century. As time passed, the service was retained to honor the memory of all Jewish martyrs, and eventually was extended to include all the Jewish dead. During the eighteenth century, a Yizkor service was added to the three joyful pilgrimage festivals called the *shelosh regalim;* on the last day of Pesach, and at the end of Shavuot and Sukkot, on Shemini Atzeret.[16] While the Yom Kippur Yizkor service is universally observed, not all liberal congregations hold Yizkor services on all three festivals.

Like any regular memorial observance, whether it happens

once a year or four times a year, Yizkor is a benchmark on the mourner's journey.[17] Saying Yizkor during festive holidays is also a way to mitigate the guilt that mourners sometimes feel as they commemorate the cycles of the year without their loved one.

Some people light a memorial candle before sunset of holidays when Yizkor is recited. As with a *yahrzeit* candle, there is no special blessing—just a moment to remember. (See pp. 149–50 for more about lighting memorial candles.) The lights beside the memorial plaques in the synagogue are also lit for Yizkor—all of them together.

Finally, Yizkor is observed by giving *tzedakah* in memory of the deceased, as pledged in the prayer. According to the rabbis, the *mitzvah* of giving to the poor is "as important as all the other commandments put together."[18]

TZEDAKAH

Tzedakah[19]—righteous giving—is a way to make memory tangible in the world. Giving money to organizations and causes that were important to the deceased keeps their beliefs alive and active. *Tzedakah* connects the living and the dead in the work of *tikkun olam*—repairing the world. "By performing [a] *mitzvah* on someone's behalf, we become that person's feet on earth."[20]

Indeed, Jewish tradition views charity as the strongest force in the universe; even greater than death itself.

Rabbi Judah used to say: Ten strong things have been created in the world. The rock of the mountain is hard, but iron cleaves it. Iron is hard, but fire softens it. Fire is powerful, but water quenches it. Water is heavy, but clouds bear it. Clouds are thick, but wind scatters them. Wind is strong, but a body resists it. A body is strong, but fear crushes it. Fear is powerful but wine banishes it. Wine is strong, but sleep works it off. Death is stronger than all, yet charity delivers from death.

As it is written, "Charity delivereth from Death."[21]

Jewish folk tradition took this proverb literally; according to ancient belief, the dead spent eleven or twelve months being judged or atoning for sins in preparation for entry into Paradise. While in this state of limbo, *tzedakah* given in the name of the deceased was thought to hasten the redemption of the soul.

Mourners promise to give memorial *tzedakah* every time they recite the Yizkor prayer. The pledge reminds the bereaved of their obligation to the living, even when weeping for the dead. The rabbis warned against excessive mourning. Helping to repair the world is a way to translate grief into healing and justice, *tzedek*.

GIVING MONEY: Jewish mourners give money to a wide variety of charities and organizations. Most people make gifts that reflect the values and interests of the person who died. Obviously, a person who volunteered and contributed to a particular organization, such as the United Jewish Appeal, or their synagogue, or the American Cancer Society, is honored by donations to "their" cause. By the same token, a passionate reader might be honored by supporting the synagogue library, the local public library, and literacy programs.

Mourners and guests who were moved by the clergy's eulogy or assistance sometimes send a check to the rabbi's discretionary fund, along with a thank-you note.

TWELVE OCCASIONS
FOR MEMORIAL *TZEDAKAH*

On hearing news of a death
On returning home from a funeral
After paying a *shiva* visit
On attending or hearing of an unveiling
On a *yahrzeit*
On visiting a cemetery
After Yizkor services
Before every Shabbat
Every time you say Kaddish
On the birthday of a loved one who has died
On attending a wedding, bar mitzvah, or *brit*
Whenever a loved one's favorite charity sends a
    solicitation[22]

BEYOND MONEY: Mourners can keep their loved ones' values and beliefs alive in the world by committing time and effort to a worthy cause. From volunteering in the soup kitchen where she used to work, to welcoming out-of-towners visiting sick relatives in the hospital, to setting up a synagogue bereavement support group, helping others embodies the Jewish idea or principle of *gemilut hassadim*—acts of loving-kindness. The Talmud has high praise for such efforts: "He who gives a coin to a poor man is rewarded with six blessings. But he who encourages him with friendly words is rewarded with eleven."[23]

The tradition singles out six particular acts as *gemilut hasadim:* providing clothes for the naked, visiting the sick, comforting mourners, accompanying the dead to the grave, providing for brides, and offering hospitality to strangers.[24] These deeds are considered especially holy because, according to rabbinic legend, God performed them for human beings. In the Midrash, God attended Eve at her wedding to Adam, comforted Isaac as he mourned for his father, and buried Moses.[25]

Mourners who are attracted to the idea of donating time as a *mitzvah* of remembrance should choose a labor of love and not a penance. If you hate answering phones, don't volunteer for a phonathon, even if it's a cause you hold dear; find another way to serve.

Three of the six acts of *gemilut hasadim* are particularly resonant for mourners: visiting the sick, comforting mourners, and showing respect for the dead. Bereaved people who found consolation in Jewish tradition and within their communities sometimes wish to "return the favor" by getting involved in programs and committees directed toward other mourners, or even starting new programs for unmet needs. For example, a person who felt completely unprepared to mourn Jewishly might help organize adult education programs about the Jewish traditions for death and mourning.

People who volunteer for these kinds of programs usually have firsthand experience of loss. Working with others who understand the ongoing process of grief can be a source of fellowship and comfort as well as a real blessing to those in immediate need. (See "Taking Comfort" in Chapter 5, and "Bibliography and Resources.")

MEMORIALS: PUBLIC AND PRIVATE

Memory is a visible part of Jewish architecture. Virtually every Jewish space—synagogue, school, community center, hospital, federation building, *mikvah*—is hung with plaques that read, "In memory of." Jewish names adorn hospitals, libraries, and university buildings, too.

Public testimonials come in all shapes and sizes, from bronze plaques hung outside classrooms, to bookplates pasted inside *siddurim* (prayer books), to five-foot-high letters chiseled in marble. Indeed, the number of plaques in Jewish buildings has, over the years, raised eyebrows and hackles. "Naming opportunities" can seem self-aggrandizing, especially since Jewish tradition prizes anonymous gifts above all.[26]

The Jewish mandate to give *tzedakah* is, of course, reason enough to donate to worthy causes. But for mourners, public memorials are also personal monuments. There is consolation in seeing a loved one's name attached to a building where children are learning from Jewish texts, or where sick people are receiving lifesaving treatment. The names of loved ones make possible innumerable quiet epiphanies about how the dead really are "bound up in the bonds of life":

At my daughter's bat mitzvah, one of her friends opened a prayer book and saw in it the name of our first child, who died in infancy. This child was so excited, she showed it to Sarah, whose eyes filled with tears and who showed it to me and her father. It seemed so right to us all.

Bricks and mortar are not the only ways to build a public memorial to a loved one. Given Judaism's emphasis on learning, people also endow academic chairs at universities and seminaries in honor of their loved ones. Some Jewish federations permit donors to earmark funds for "named" endowments in areas of particular interest, such as education or outreach.

Endowed memorial lectures are becoming increasingly popular. In the past, when a great rabbi died, his students would hold a *shiur,* or class, to mark the anniversary of his death and to keep his teachings alive. Following this tradition, mourners can endow a fund whose annual interest pays for a lecture or adult education series. The family gathers for these events, which begin with a few words that recall the person in whose name the occasion was made possible.

Thus, one temple sponsors an annual lecture on Jewish humor in memory of a mother who loved laughter. A college Hillel holds an annual lecture in honor of a faculty member who was instrumental in supporting the campus Jewish student center. A local federation holds an event for young people in memory of a daughter who died in her twenties. Not all memorials cost money. Mourners create personal "monuments" within their families and in their own lives.

STUDY: The most traditional personal memorial is making a commitment to Jewish study. For Jews who do not usually attend services, going to weekly Shabbat services or daily *minyan* may be a multifaceted learning experience, including exposure to liturgy, Hebrew reading skills, and a new connection to the community. In some circles, mourners are given the option of leading some part of the daily minyan or reading from the Torah as the anniversary of the death approaches—an honor that becomes a goal.

Some mourners, inspired or intrigued by exposure to Jewish

mourning customs, embark on a course of Jewish reading, either on their own or under the direction of a rabbi, cantor, or other teacher. Other mourners sign up for Jewish adult education courses.

MEMORY BOOKS: In Israel, the custom of putting together a *hoveret*, or memorial pamphlet, is a common practice, especially in memory of young people who died in the armed forces. A memory book can include photographs, newspaper clippings, documents, letters written by and to the deceased, poems written in their memory, pictures of children and grandchildren—anything that illustrates the person's life. These are often photocopied, bound, and distributed to family members. When grandparents die, special care is taken to give each grandchild his or her own copy of the book.

NAMES: The most common and perhaps the most profound "living memorial" is the custom of naming children in memory of the dead. At most *brit milah* and *brit habat* ceremonies— covenant ceremonies for baby boys and girls—it is now customary for one or both parents to explain the choice of the name, and tell stories about the person (or people) whose memory is embodied in the baby's name.

Ashkenazic Jews name children after relatives who have passed away. This custom is based on an East European superstition that the angel of death might make a mistake and take a child instead of an older relative with the same name. While the superstition is largely forgotten, the custom is deeply entrenched and beloved.[27]

Often, names are simply handed down: Aunt Ruth's memory lives on in her grandniece, Ruth. But it is also customary for parents to give their baby the same Hebrew name as the person honored and select a secular name on the basis of the initial letter or sound of the Hebrew. Which is how it happens that Grandpa Moshe's grandson will be called to the Torah for his bar mitzvah as "Moshe" but on the playground will answer to "Max."

POEM FOR
BRIT MILAH OR *BRIT HABAT*

We give you an old name,
A beloved name, a crown.
We give you a name to honor the past,
A promise to the future,
Yours to make new.

B'shem avotenu v' imotenu
In the name of all our fathers and mothers,
And in memory of _____,
Your name is a gift of the ages.
B'shem avotenu v' imotenu
In the name of all our fathers and mothers,
We will call you _____,
A name that is yours alone.

ANITA DIAMANT

....

CHAPTER TEN

PARTICULAR
LOSSES

CHILDREN AS MOURNERS, NEONATAL DEATH, MOURNING for non-Jews, suicide—though different in many ways, mourners who confront these losses often share a sense of being disenfranchised. Children's grief may be overlooked or denied in the name of "protecting" them from sadness; pregnancy loss is often kept secret; mourners for non-Jewish loved ones feel caught between traditions; suicide leaves an overwhelming burden of guilt.

The traditional response to such losses was not always helpful or healing; the trauma of miscarriage, for example, is barely acknowledged by Jewish law or custom. However, by reinterpreting and reconstructing ancient rituals in light of contemporary wisdom, liberal Jews are creating new traditions that are both respectful of the past and true to contemporary insights. Women's experience informs new rituals for prenatal and neonatal loss, and developmental psychology guides the care of bereaved children with heightened awareness of their needs as mourners.

CHILDREN AS MOURNERS

A teacher dies of cancer. A schoolmate is killed in a car accident.

A grandfather dies and his nine-year-old granddaughter sees her mother held and comforted by many friends. The girl's father devotes his attention to her grieving mother. "Nobody asks me how I'm feeling," she says, with angry tears. "I'm sad, too. He was my grandfather."

Even when a child's sibling or parent dies, adult grief tends to overshadow the feelings of younger mourners.

According to Jewish tradition, children under the age of thirteen are not required to observe the rituals of mourning. They are not obliged to accompany the body to the grave, or to be present for *shiva* services. The exemption does not mean that children are prohibited from attending or taking part, but for many years adults behaved as though there were such a prohibition. It used to be common practice to keep children far from the funerals, *shiva* services, and unveilings that might have helped give shape and meaning to grief.

The impulse to shield children from death is so strong it feels instinctive. Some people take refuge in the notion that the young can't understand what's going on around them. In fact, that is not the case. Child psychologists, grief experts, and rabbis agree that children need and deserve to hear the truth about death, and whenever appropriate, they need and deserve to be included in mourning rituals.

Caring for bereaved children is always sad and often confusing. It is difficult for adults, usually in pain themselves, to witness the suffering of children. But without the truth, the young are left to fend for themselves in the valley of the shadow. Although every child and every loss is different, there are a few general guidelines to keep in mind:

DON'T DELAY: News of a death should be delivered by a parent or other trusted adult as soon as possible. Waiting won't soften the blow and increases the chances that the child will learn what happened in an inappropriate setting. Even the best of intentions can backfire: "If we wait until after camp to tell Rina about Bubby's death, we won't ruin her summer." In that case, Rina will be mourning all by herself when she learns the news.

AVOID EUPHEMISMS: Use the words "dead" and "death." Terms like "passed away" or "eternal rest" are confusing to children who are trying to grapple with the finality of what has happened. A young child who hears the words "We lost Grandma" might believe that she may yet be found.

Explain what happened to the person who died, being careful in your choice of words. Saying "Grandpa died because he was sick" or "Grandma died in the hospital" can create the fear that all illness leads to death or all hospital stays are fatal. For a child under the age of eight, a term like "heart attack" may be confusing or even frightening.

While there is no need to be graphic, be as specific as possible: "Grandma's heart stopped working. Lots of times, doctors can help people with sick hearts get better, but sometimes, especially when people are very old, there is no medicine that works. That is why she died."

INVITE QUESTIONS: Some children will be able to express their curiosity and ask about everything from bodily decomposition to the existence of heaven. But don't assume that silence means a lack of interest. Some children do not ask because they lack the words, or out of confusion, or for fear of upsetting adults.

Make time when children know they have your undivided attention and solicit their questions in specific terms. "Is there anything you'd like to ask me about the funeral?" "Would you like me to tell you about Grandpa's last words?" Remember that even children who refuse to ask need to know the facts.

Not all questions are easy to answer. "What happens to your eyeballs after you die?" "Why can't I have my birthday party this week?" "Will Uncle Al go to heaven now?" "Is Susan going to be an angel?" "Why did God let this happen to a baby?"

Acknowledge the importance of such questions. Talk about how you answer them for yourself, or perhaps say a little about how Jews have answered them through history. Admit that you're still struggling for answers. Don't be afraid to say, "I don't know."

Another good response to any perplexing question is, "That's a very good question. What do you think?" Very often, children may need this kind of opening to express what's really on their minds.

Above all, be honest, offer reassurance, and show affection.

REMEMBER THAT CHILDREN GRIEVE IN THEIR OWN WAYS: Some will weep and cling, others will run outside to play with friends, and still others will go back and forth between sorrow and apparent indifference. Some children "act out," regressing to earlier stages of development; others become hostile or demanding or timid.

Whether or not they can express their feelings, death is profoundly disturbing to children. And whatever they say or do, children need to know that their feelings and moods aren't right or wrong, but simply normal. An adult can help a child name the conflicting emotions that tend to come up. "You know, I've been feeling so many things since your sister died. I'm so sad but I'm also angry that she isn't here anymore, that I won't get to see her again, and that our family has been changed so much."

Sometimes children need to hear that even grown-ups feel guilty about mean things they said or nice things they didn't say. Or that adults feel relieved after long illness and suffering are finally over.

GIVE CHILDREN A WAY TO SAY GOOD-BYE: Funerals are for everyone who cared about the deceased. Children who are kept away from funerals often imagine scenes far more gruesome and terrible than the real thing. They may also feel that their grief is being ignored. Even young children can be included for short periods of time and taken out of the room when they can no longer sit still or remain quiet.

It's important for parents who are bereaved to ask a relative or close friend to attend to children at the funeral. A bereaved daughter should not feel responsible for her own children at her mother's funeral; she needs to be a daughter in mourning.

Most school-age children can make informed choices about attending or participating in mourning rituals. Parents should describe what is going to happen at a funeral or *shiva* house: who will be there, the fact that people may be weeping. Explain how long the service or visit will last and offer options. (For a discussion of ways to include children during the first seven days of mourning, see Chapter 7, "Shiva.")

Nevertheless, children should also have the right to opt out of rituals. A child who clearly states she doesn't want to go to a funeral, to the cemetery, or to pay a *shiva* visit shouldn't be dragged along or made to feel ashamed of her choice.

SHARE YOUR FEELINGS: Children watch adults for cues about how to manage their emotions. If adults cry and console one another, children learn that it's normal and safe to express emotion. However, since children can be frightened by the sight of weeping adults, they also need specific reassurance. A weeping parent can say: "Daddy is very sad, but I'm going to be okay. Crying is just part of what happens when someone you love dies."

IT TAKES A VILLAGE: Bereaved children benefit just as much as bereaved adults from being part of a community of comforters. Since parents and other close relatives are usually suffering from the same loss, they may be understandably less able to focus on the individual needs of each child. Friends and neighbors, baby-sitters and teachers, cousins and in-laws, can help by spending time with children, encouraging their questions, or giving them breaks from the rest of the family's grief.

A bereaved child's teachers should be fully informed so they can sympathize, inform classmates, and be alert to changes in behavior.

BOOKS: Reading aloud to prereaders is a good way to start conversations and keep track of a child's developing understanding of what happened. Children old enough to read can look at books that speak to their interests and anxieties. There are scores of titles for children of all ages, some of which focus on specific kinds of losses, including the death of a grandparent, parent, or sibling.

Your rabbi or child's teacher may have some recommendations, and children's librarians will be able to direct you to new releases as well as classics and to tailor suggestions to a child's reading level. Many funeral homes provide pamphlets or books for parents and children.

It's a good idea for parents or guardians to read any book before giving it to a child, both to make sure it is age-appropriate and that it reflects the family's values and beliefs.

Another kind of book to give a bereaved child is a memory book. Published memory workbooks include questions and places for photographs and drawings; however, any notebook or diary can fulfill the same purpose. Some children want to share what they write in these books; others do not. That decision should be left to the child.

SEEKING PROFESSIONAL HELP: Some children are overwhelmed by grief and need a therapist's help. Adults should consider this possibility for any child who has suffered a loss within his nuclear family.

Be alert to signs of depression such as sleep disorders, listlessness, or uncontrollable tears. Children or teens may have panic attacks, show a decline in schoolwork over time, or continue to deny that the death ever happened. Sometimes, symptoms are delayed, making it harder for parents and other adults to connect behavior changes to the loss.

School counselors are generally the first line of professional assistance. A few sessions with the guidance counselor or school psychologist may be all that's needed to help a child sort out her feelings. Just knowing there is a concerned but dispassionate adult to talk to can be enormously comforting for a bereaved child. If problems persist, the school counselor may provide a referral to a specialist. Referrals can also come from your rabbi or pediatrician, the local Jewish chaplaincy organization, healing center, or hospice rabbi.

Young mourners need specialized care and treatment. When interviewing counselors, ask about their experience working with bereaved children. Have they taken courses in the field? Are they members of the Association for Death Education and Counseling? Listen to what your child has to say, too. If after two or three sessions, he or she puts up a fight over going, it might be time to find another counselor.

AGES AND STAGES: Words and ideas don't have the same meaning for three-year-olds and ten-year-olds, nor are they the same for all three-year-olds or all ten-year-olds. Since children develop at differing rates and sometimes regress during times of stress, the following descriptions are only general and schematic.

Under Three: Infants and toddlers do not understand death, but they are sensitive to disruption of routines and changes in the emotional climate, and a house full of strangers may be upsetting. When death is in the house, little ones need even more attention than usual and lots of physical affection.

Infants and toddlers can light up the room when people are in mourning; their presence is a reminder of why life must go on. However, fussy or rambunctious babies do not belong in the room during a funeral or a *shiva* service.

Three-to-Six-Year-Olds: Children vary enormously at this age both in terms of what they understand and how they respond. Some young children cry and cling, which is perfectly normal. Others appear unaffected, and this is perfectly normal, too.

Some won't be able to focus on the idea at first; death is simply too strange, foreign, and frightening. Others will be fascinated and ask uninhibited questions about exactly where the dead person is, what she is doing, and perhaps when she will be back. The idea of permanence, of "forever," is virtually incomprehensible at this age. Children sometimes appear to deny or forget that the dead person is really dead, and may need several gentle repetitions of the facts.

Preschoolers tend to be literal-minded, and thus most vulnerable to euphemisms about death. The idea that a loved one is "asleep" can be translated into bedtime terrors. Talking about how the dead are "up in the clouds" may lead to vain hopes of actually seeing them again. This is the age when talking about the "loss" of a grandparent prompts suggestions about going out to "find" him.

Death may be terrifying to many young children, who become fearful about losing other adults in their lives. Parents may be asked, "Are you going to die?" Knowing that everyone dies eventually and wanting to be honest makes this a very hard question. One way to answer is: "Most people live to be old before they die. I expect to be alive and well for a long, long time."

Young children sometimes believe they caused a death by wishing someone harm. Adults should offer reassurance that the child had nothing to do with it, even if he came right out and said, "I wish you were dead." Although it's not necessary to go into great detail, children need reasonable explanations to allay their fears. Tell the truth. "Aunt Jenny died because of a disease called cancer."

Whether or not they explicitly give voice to fears and feelings, young children need verbal reassurance that they are safe and things will be okay. They also need lots of physical affection.

Seven-to-Eleven-Year-Olds: By this stage, children start to understand that death is final, which means that their fears may come into sharper focus. Questions about the mechanics of illness can become more pointed. Some want to hear all the "gory details" about what happens to the body after death. Others might demand an explanation of how God could let such an awful thing happen.

The imagination is still a powerful force among children of this age, who might envision death as a kind of scary bogeyman, or fear that death is somehow contagious. While they may consciously "know" that their own words or wishes did not really cause a death, school-age children may not fully believe this and feel miserably guilty about something they said or thought. Some suffer over unkindness shown to the deceased. Parents and guardians need to reassure their children and absolve them of any guilt they may be feeling.

Some children at this age are able to attend and even participate in mourning rituals. If asked, they can write a letter or poem to or about the person who died; this can be included in the funeral or at a *shiva* service. This option is not for everyone. Shy children should never be forced to participate.

Memory books can be a good project for school-age children. While a simple notebook will do, there are published pamphlets and workbooks that help kids focus on their own feelings as well as on the life of the person who died.[1]

As with adults, grief can take older children on an emotional roller coaster: from weepy to apparently stoic, from clingy to withdrawn. They need reassurance that everything they are feeling is normal.

Adolescents: Death hits teenagers very hard. Cognitively, adolescents understand the finality of death, but few teens are able to tolerate the intensity of their feelings. Unlike younger kids, adolescents may have begun to move out from under the protective emotional umbrella provided by their parents.

Loss poses a developmental quandary for teens, who are normally engaged in the process of separating from parents. Loss shatters a new and still-fragile sense of independence and forces adolescents back into needing adults—parents in particular. The normal push-pull of adolescence is intensified and often takes the form of anger.

Parents' best strategy is to seek a balance between their teenagers' need for independence and their equally important need for limits. Sometimes, it's easier if another grown-up—an uncle, aunt, neighbor, or teacher—can act as the adult sounding board in the aftermath of a death. But peer relationships, which are crucial to teenagers, should also be seen as a source of comfort.

Adolescents often find themselves cut off from their friends at precisely the time they need them the most. Close friends should be made welcome whenever a grieving adolescent says he wants them around, including at the funeral and during *shiva*.

The privacy of "bibliotheraphy" may appeal to young people. Books that articulate the anguish of grief—especially poetry and fiction—can be a source of release and comfort. This is also a time to encourage self-expression, and some teens appreciate the gift of a special diary or bound notebook for keeping track of the journey through sorrow.

DEVELOPMENTAL GRIEF: As children mature, they grow into new levels of understanding about death and how they are connected to loved ones who died. At every stage, new questions may surface, new feelings arise. Bereaved children—especially those who lost a parent or sibling—encounter the hole in their lives every birthday and holiday. This may be true even if they have no memory of the deceased.

Family members and other adults do well to encourage questions by demonstrating their willingness to talk about the deceased:

"Daddy would have loved seeing you in that dress."

"Grandma would have been so proud of you today."

"What do you think your big sister would have thought of this?"

"Did I ever tell you the story about when my brother, your Uncle Joe, caught the biggest fish in the lake?"

When adults reminisce, they should also solicit the child's memories: "What do you remember most about Grandma?"

In addition to talking about the deceased, participating in Jewish memorial events helps children feel a personal connection to the loved one. Children can be encouraged to collect and arrange photographs around Grandma's *yahrzeit* candle, or to read the letter Uncle Max wrote before he died. They can also be offered the option of standing for the mourner's Kaddish, or given the honor of choosing where to send a charitable donation in memory of the deceased.

As children grow, these acts take on different meanings. And as time passes, the candles and the stories themselves fulfill the hope of the Yizkor prayer, "May his/her memory be bound up in the bonds of life."[2]

MOURNING NON-JEWISH LOVED ONES

The religious, ethnic, and cultural boundaries of the Jewish community today are as permeable as they have ever been. Liberal

Jews routinely count non-Jews not only among their closest friends, but also as members of their families. Increases in inter-marriage and conversion since the 1970s raise questions about many aspects of family and community life, including how to mourn for non-Jewish loved ones.

Although Jewish tradition has relatively little to say about mourning for non-Jews, the subject is hardly new. Throughout history, Jews have grieved for gentile friends, neighbors, and business associates. According to Jewish law, accompanying the body of a non-Jew to the cemetery was considered an appropriate show of respect. Rabbi Maurice Lamm, a contemporary Orthodox authority on death and mourning, says that Kaddish may be recited, "at the graveside of a worthy gentile."[3]

Conversion to Judaism is an age-old part of the Jewish community, which means that Jews-by-choice have always mourned members of their non-Jewish family of origin, though often privately.[4] Even in the contemporary atmosphere of welcome and openness about conversion, Jews-by-choice and their families are sometimes at a loss about how to express their grief in meaningfully Jewish ways.

Converts are not obliged to say Kaddish or observe other mourning rituals for non-Jewish relatives; however, the tradition has always been emphatic about the importance of showing respect for one's family of origin, especially parents.[5] Liberal Jews who have lost a non-Jewish loved one usually attend non-Jewish funerals, wakes, and visiting hours.[6]

The whole range of Jewish mourning customs is open to any Jew mourning for a non-Jew. Converts say Kaddish for their non-Jewish parents at daily or weekly services. The loss of a non-Jewish friend prompts some Jews to light a candle on the anniversary of his death. Of course, any synagogue member can request bereavement counseling from his or her rabbi, regardless of the deceased's religion. In some congregations, there are occasional workshops and discussion groups about bereavement and mourning customs for converts and their families.

There are, however, some questions that transcend strictly personal choices. For example:

- Where does an intermarried couple buy a burial plot?
- How does the rabbi respond when a member of his congregation asks him to officiate at the nonsectarian funeral of her mother, a nominal but nonpracticing Protestant?
- Will the synagogue's cemetery permit the interment of a lifelong member of the congregation who never made his conversion formal?
- Can a rabbi offer a prayer or eulogy at the church funeral of a congregant's non-Jewish husband?
- Will the name of a convert's non-Jewish family member be included in the Yizkor list of names published for Yom Kippur?
- Can a charitable contribution made in memory of a non-Jewish parent be memorialized by a brass plaque in the temple?

These are questions that rabbis and synagogues answer in a wide range of ways and often on a case-by-case basis. They are certainly fodder for congregational debate and evidence of the changing nature of the community as a whole.

Other questions and concerns are far more intimate than institutional and, unfortunately, tend to leave mourners feeling isolated just when community is most needed. For example:

- A Jew-by-choice from a large Catholic family is told that his mother's wake will include an open casket. Can he raise objections to the practice? Can he refuse to attend the wake without giving offense? Is it meaningful to sit *shiva* without his siblings?
- Another convert finds herself shut out of the planning for her brother's funeral; she feels like a guest rather than a mourner at the funeral. Back in her own congregation, she doesn't know if she is "entitled" to sit *shiva,* or how to ask for support.
- A non-Jewish synagogue member asks his rabbi if she would bury him, to which the rabbi replies, "I only know how to bury Jews."

Family dynamics, personalities, and synagogue custom determine how situations like these are resolved. But while every loss is unique, community support remains the keystone of the Jewish response to bereavement. Mourners who feel marginalized because of religious difference should know that the issues facing all mourners—regardless of religious background—are more similar than different.

For example, the disagreements that divide interfaith families are not all that different from the ones that cause conflict in all-Jewish or all-Christian families. Most extended families are split over religious observance and practice: some members are more traditional than others; some are affiliated while others are not. Likewise, the sense of feeling split geographically as well as religiously is a common phenomenon in the Jewish community. Holding rituals and observances that meet the needs of different branches of the family, often in different cities, is common practice.

A death can expose unreconciled issues, profound differences, and old tensions within any family. If there has been a conversion or intermarriage, old feelings of abandonment and loss may rise to the surface. Your rabbi can act as a thoughtful sounding board at such a time. He or she may have seen other mourners through similar problems. Likewise, it may be a good idea to talk to other Jews-by-choice or members of interfaith families with similar experiences; no one else is better able to empathize with the "betwixt and between" feelings and help ease the loneliness. A rabbi or cantor may be able to help identify other bereaved Jews-by-choice or interfaith families in the congregation.

DAYENU

When I die, my children will say
Kaddish for me and that, with pinewood box
and linen shroud, will be enough.

In time, I will say Kaddish
for my parents. It will not be enough.
They believe in Hell's Yellow Emperor,
fret about food, shelter for their ghosts.
The magnification of an alien God's name
would send them into the afterlife, barefoot
ghosts on hard dirt streets, banging
tin cups on red doors. They would drink
bitter tea, lie alongside ghosts with unopened wombs.

So I have promised my mother I will burn
a paper mansion with puppet servants, chests
of paper gold, paper shells of cars.
My brothers will provide oolong
and chicken rice each feast day, the monthly
stipend of Hell money, shells of faith.
These we render to our mother who tied
red thread on our feet and fingers as we slid
from her womb to bind us to life.

We hold this end of the scarlet thread
our parents unravel as they near the Yellow Springs,
feel it tighten as the wind
blowing off the river, lodges dust in our eyes.

HILARY THAM[7]

191

STILLBIRTH, NEONATAL LOSS, MISCARRIAGE

The howl of pain and disbelief that attends these losses is as ancient as human life. The Zohar, the thirteenth-century text of Jewish mysticism, cries out against the wrongness of infant death:

> But the most grievous is the sorrow surrounding those "oppressed ones" who as still sucklings are taken from their mother's breast. On their account truly, the whole world weeps; the tears that come from these babies have no equal, their tears issue from the innermost and farthest places of the heart, and the entire world is perplexed and says: Eternally righteous are the judgments of the Holy One, be blessed, and all Adonai's paths are paths of truth. Yet, is it needful that these unhappy infants should die, who are without sin and without blame? In this, where is the rightful and just judgment of the Lord of the World?[8]

Burying a child of any age is agony. A death so close to birth seems like the loss of hope itself. Bereaved mothers and fathers can tell you that they are never the same after losing a child. Not after 15 years or fifty years. Never.

Like bereaved children who grieve in different ways as they mature, bereaved parents also experience a kind of "developmental" mourning. On every uncelebrated birthday and missed milestone, grief takes on new dimensions. Support is crucial, yet parents of miscarried or stillborn children, and of babies who die within months of birth, are "disenfranchised mourners." Many would-be comforters are confounded and frightened by the magnitude of the loss; they don't know what to say, or say nothing, or worst of all, make thoughtless comments about "trying again."

Until recently, Jewish tradition offered little solace. Although the physical remains of miscarriage, stillbirth, or neonatal loss were treated with the utmost respect, public forms of mourning were discouraged. No funeral was held and parents did not sit *shiva* or say Kaddish.[9] This was not intended to be cruel. During the centuries when infant mortality was high, the rabbis may have meant to spare parents the burdens and obligations of official mourning.

Today, however, when prenatal and neonatal death are relatively rare, the absence of Jewish ritual feels like another blow to already shattered hearts. In keeping with current medical and psychological practice, which encourages parents to view and hold their infants after death and to actively mourn their loss, Jewish custom has changed dramatically.

Graveside funerals for infants are now very common; some funeral homes and cemeteries provide the casket and plot without cost. Parents decide to sit *shiva* either for one, three, or the full seven days. Rabbis advise bereaved parents to get counseling, or join a pregnancy loss or stillbirth support group; they may also be able to introduce members of the congregation who have suffered similar losses. Obstetricians and rabbis can make referrals to local agencies and counselors.

God, we are weary and grieved. We anticipated the birth of a child, but the promise of life has ended too soon. Our arms yearned to cradle new life, our mouths to sing soft lullabies. Our hearts ache from the emptiness and the silence. We are saddened and we are angry. We weep and we mourn. Weep with us, God, creator of life, for the life that could not be sustained.

Source of healing, help us to find healing among those who care for us and for whom we care. Shelter us under the wings of love and help us to stand up again for life even as we mourn our loss.

בָּרוּךְ אַתָּה יהוה אֱלֹהֵינוּ מֶלֶךְ הָעוֹלָם
זוֹכֵר יְצוּרָיו לְחַיִּים בְּרַחֲמִים:

Baruch ata Adonai, Elohenu melech ha-olam
Zocher yet-zu-rav le-cha-yim be-rachamim

Blessed are you, Eternal, who remembers with compassion those you have created for life.[10]

MISCARRIAGE: As many as 20 percent of conceptions end in miscarriage. Pregnancy loss can be a devastating death of a dream whenever it occurs, and especially so for couples who have struggled to conceive.

Although the pain of infertility was given eloquent voice in the Bible,[11] until recently Jewish tradition remained silent about the loss associated with it. While miscarriage still tends to be a very private experience, the silence has been broken by rabbis and liturgists—many of them women—who understand the need to name and mourn this loss.

PRAYER AFTER A MISCARRIAGE

יְחִידוֹ שֶׁל עוֹלָם *Y'chido shel-olam,* Holy One of Being,
source of all life and destiny of all souls, receive the soul
of this one that was not-yet-a-life but only a dream. Send
us healing in our grief and confusion. Give us strength
and the ability to look for a future again filled with new
life and new dreams. Let hopeful parents everywhere,
who have known the agony of loss, be soon comforted by
the sounds of a baby's cry.

RABBI LAWRENCE KUSHNER

SUICIDE

Suicide leaves behind an overwhelming roster of emotions: anger, guilt, embarrassment, shame. Isolation, confusion, rejection, abandonment, desertion. Failure, despair.

Suicide leaves mourners even more isolated than other kinds of losses. Words of condolence, while never easy, seem even more difficult to find.

Judaism has always viewed suicide with horror. Not only was it viewed as an act of violence on a par with murder; self-destruction was considered religious sacrilege, a desecration of creation and a rejection of the Holy One who creates life and decrees death.[12]

The law prohibiting self-destruction led to sanctions against observance of many Jewish mourning rites. In the past, mourners of a suicide were not permitted to rend their clothing and no eulogy was delivered at the funeral. Making the choice of cutting oneself off from life was further "punished" by prohibitions against burying suicides with the rest of the community. They were interred either just outside the Jewish cemetery, at its perimeter, or in a separate area designated for suicides.

While the community was encouraged to comfort the bereaved by accompanying them to the cemetery and visiting them at home, the prohibitions inevitably isolated mourners and compounded their pain. This fact concerned the rabbis, who, over time, defined suicide in narrower and narrower terms. Eventually, only someone who killed himself out of "a cynical disregard for life" was judged a suicide; someone who ended his life out of despair was not.[13]

Today, the Jewish community treats suicide as a symptom of clinical depression or mental illness, which means no distinction is made in how they are mourned or buried. The bereaved perform *k'riah*, eulogies are delivered, and cemeteries no longer restrict the burial of suicides.[14]

Whatever the official communal response, however, mourners are staggered by guilt and self-blame: Why didn't I see the signs? What was it about me that kept her from confiding in me? And there is guilt about the inevitable anger directed at the deceased: anger at being abandoned and anger at the physical, psychological, legal, and financial messes that suicide leaves behind.

Suicide is usually a manifestation of mental illness, and no one is to blame for it. Nevertheless, a medical explanation alone cannot provide emotional closure or solace or a way out of the terrible guilt. For this to happen, suicide survivors need to find acceptance and forgiveness.

Accepting the fact that the deceased took his or her own life is a profound loss in its own right. It means acknowledging the separateness of each human being and recognizing the limits of love.

Forgiveness works in two directions. Survivors have to forgive the deceased for the damage he or she did to others. Recalling the role of mental illness and/or despair in the death can help mourners turn away from blame and remember the dead with compassion.

Self-forgiveness, which is just as important, is probably more difficult. Poring over the past, mourners often remember times when they missed "warnings" that seem clear in hindsight. Of course, everyone misses opportunities to reach out and help—usually on a daily basis. Most of the time, though, those lapses can be redressed; apologies can be made and accepted. Most of the time, there are second chances.

Suicide closes the door on second chances, leaving the mourner to face an agony of regret. Forgiving yourself and accepting that what happened was beyond your control takes a long time, and often requires help from a counselor or a support group.

Not all suicides are acts of mental illness or despair, as when a person who is terminally ill or facing intractable pain decides to end her life. While the issue is hardly new, life-prolonging medical advances have made this choice more common.

Such cases are always embedded in the myriad particulars of personality, prognosis, family dynamics, and mental health. While there are differences between deciding to forgo intubation and taking an overdose of sleeping pills, the aftermath for mourners can be equally agonizing. Should I have argued with him? Should I have ignored the medical directive?

Jewish tradition and law tend to oppose choices that shorten life, though not in every case. (See pp. 37–39.) Rabbis frequently support dying patients and their families in decisions to end or limit treatment, even knowing that the end will come sooner as a result.

Whatever your situation, it is good to remember that others have faced similar losses. Most congregational rabbis, hospital chaplains, and hospice rabbis have some experience with "passive" suicide and "self-deliverance" and the grief that follows. There is no reason to mourn in shame or isolation.[15]

EIGHT MORE WAYS TO SAY KADDISH

TRANSLATIONS

....

THE ORPHAN'S KADDISH

May it be magnified
and may it be sanctified,
God's great name, **Amen!***

in the world whose creation God willed.
May God's dominion be fulfilled

in your life
and in your days
and in the life of the whole House of Israel,

soon and near in time,
and say, **Amen!**

**May God's great name be praised
forever, and ever and ever!**

May it be praised
and may it be blessed
and may it be honored
and may it be upraised
and may it be elevated,

may it be glorified
and may it be exalted
and may it be extolled,

---

* *Boldface denotes congregational response.*

the name of the Holy One,
Praised be God!

beyond all words-of-praise, words-of-song,
words-of-blessing, and words-of-comfort
that can be uttered in this world,
and say, **Amen!**

May there be great peace from heaven
and life
for us and for all Israel,
and say, **Amen!**

Maker of peace in the abode-on-high,
may God make peace
for us and for all Israel,
and say, **Amen!**

EVERETT FOX (AFTER FRANZ ROSENZWEIG)[1]

Hallowed and enhanced may He be throughout the world of His own creation. May God cause His sovereignty to be accepted during our life and the life of all Israel. And let us say: Amen.

May He be praised throughout all time.

Glorified and celebrated, lauded and praised, acclaimed and honored, extolled and exalted may the Holy One be, far beyond all song and psalm, beyond all tribute which man can utter. And let us say: Amen.

Let there be abundant peace from Heaven, with life's goodness for us and for all the people Israel. And let us say, Amen.

He who brings peace to His universe will bring peace to us and to all the people Israel. And let us say: Amen.

FROM THE *MACHZOR*
FOR ROSH HASHANAH
AND YOM KIPPUR[2]

KADDISH

Exalted and hallowed be God's greatness
In this world of Your creation.
May Your will be fulfilled
And Your sovereignty revealed
In the days of our lifetime
And the life of the whole house of Israel
Speedily and soon.
And say, Amen.

May You be blessed forever,
Even to all eternity.
May You, most Holy One, be blessed,
Praised and honored, extolled and glorified,
Adored and exalted above all else.

Blessed are You.
Beyond all blessings and hymns, praises and consolations
That may be uttered in this world
And say, Amen.

May peace abundant descend from heaven
With life for us and for all Israel,
And say, Amen.

May God, Who makes peace on high,
Bring peace to us and to all Israel,
And say, Amen.

FROM *VETAHER LIBEYNU* (PURIFY OUR HEARTS),
SIDDUR OF CONGREGATION BETH EL
OF THE SUDBURY RIVER VALLEY[3]

KADDISH

Look around us, search above us, below, behind.
We stand in a great web of being joined together.
Let us praise, let us love the life we are lent
passing through us in the body of Israel
and our own bodies, let's say amen.

Time flows through us like water.
The past and the dead speak through us.
We breathe out our children's children, blessing.

Blessed is the earth from which we grow,
blessed the life we are lent,
blessed the ones who teach us,
blessed the ones we teach,
blessed is the word that cannot say the glory
that shines through us and remains to shine
flowing past distant suns on the way to forever,
Let's say amen.

Blessed is light, blessed is darkness,
but blessed above all else is peace
which bears the fruits of knowledge
on strong branches, let's say amen.

Peace that bears joy into the world,
peace that enables love, peace over Israel
everywhere, blessed and holy is peace, let's say amen.

MARGE PIERCY[4]

KADDISH

Render greatness and holiness to the mighty name of God, throughout the world which he has created according to His will.

May His kingdom flower in your time and in the time of the whole house of Israel, quickly, soon. And to this let us say Amen.

May His mighty name be blest for eternity.

Cry laudation and honor to that holy name which is above all the praises and adorings of our world and all its consolations. And to this let us say Amen.

May our prayers be answered, may the supplications of all Israel find favor with our Father in heaven. And to this let us say Amen.

May His heavenly peace touch us, may long and good life be given to us and all Israel.

May He who establishes His peace on the heights bring peace and comforting also to us and to all Israel. And to this let us say Amen.

HYAM PLUTZIK[5]

INTRODUCTION
TO THE
KADDISH

When a soldier in the forces of a ruler of flesh and blood falls,
That ruler hardly knows that one is missing.
If one soldier is slain, there are others to replace that one.

But our Ruler, the Creator of the Universe,
The Holy One, Who is to be blessed,
Desires life, loves peace and pursues peace;
When one of Israel is missing,
A diminishing and lessening takes place;
There is a decline of strength.
Therefore we pray after the death of each Jew,
Yitgadal v'yitkadah sh'mey raba,

May the Power of the Name be magnified,
And may no lessening of power come to the Holy One
Who is blessed and sanctified,
In the world which was created according to the Holy Will.

Therefore, O sisters and brothers of the whole house of Israel,
All you who participate in this mourning,
Let us turn our hearts to the Holy One,
The Ruler and Redeemer of Israel.
And pray—for ourselves—and for our Creator as well:
That we may be worthy to live and see with our very eyes,

Oseh shalom bi-m'romav
Hu ya-aseh shalom aleynu v'al kol yisrael.
That the One, who mercifully makes peace in the heavens,
Will make peace for us,
And for all Israel.
And let us say: Amen.

ADAPTED FROM THE POEM BY S. Y. AGNON[6]

MOURNER'S KADDISH FOR EVERYDAY

Build me up of memory
loving and angry, tender and honest.
Let my loss build me a heart of wisdom,
compassion for the world's many losses.

Each hour is mortal
and each hour is eternal
and each hour is our testament.
May I create worthy memories
all the days of my life.

DEBRA CASH[7]

EACH OF US HAS A NAME

Each of us has a name
given by the source of life
and given by our parents

Each of us has a name
given by our stature and our smile
and given by what we wear

Each of us has a name
given by the mountains
and given by our walls

Each of us has a name
given by the stars
and given by our neighbors

Each of us has a name
given by our sins
and given by our longing

Each of us has a name
given by our enemies
and given by our love

Each of us has a name
given by our celebrations
and given by our work

Each of us has a name
given by the seasons
and given by our blindness

Each of us has a name
given by the sea
and given by
our death.

AFTER A POEM BY ZELDA,
ADAPTATION BY MARCIA FALK[8]

....

PLANNING
FOR THE UNTHINKABLE

HAVE YOU WRITTEN A WILL? Is there a health-care directive among your important papers? Do you own a funeral plot? Does your family know what kind of coffin you want to be buried in? Have you filled out an organ donation card? Have you written a letter that tells your loved ones how you feel about them and what you wish for them?

Talking about the logistics, legal consequences, and costs of death seems crass and cold. Regardless of your age or health, the topic is depressing and even for devout skeptics, this is a conversation designed to tempt the evil eye (*ayin hara*).

Difficult as it is, however, making arrangements for the end of life is not only prudent and an act of compassion for those left to mourn, it's also a way of facing up to the spiritual challenge of your own mortality.

WRITING A WILL

Over 70 percent of Americans do not have a will of any kind. This is a frightening statistic given the potential consequences of dying intestate—or will-less. In the absence of a will, the guardianship of minor children is left up to judges and social service agencies. When someone dies without a will, their money and property is divided and distributed according to each state's intestate succession laws, which follow formulas that divide property among a few close relatives. In the case of a married couple without children, for example, when one spouse dies, the surviving spouse may be required to split the estate with the deceased's parents. And states do not permit property to be inherited by unmarried partners, unless stipulated in a will.

The basic functions of a will are:

- to name a guardian to care for minor children and to arrange for management of property left to minors
- to designate people and/or organizations that will inherit your money and property
- to cancel debts others owe you
- to specify how debts and taxes are to be paid
- to designate an executor, someone who will oversee all the provisions of your will

Most people assume they need an attorney to draw up a will, and while that is not the case, making an appointment with a lawyer is the only way many people get it done. Legal fees for drawing up a will run the gamut from a few hundred dollars to several thousand, depending on the complexity of the will and the lawyer's hourly rate.

People with substantial wealth are generally advised to take legal steps to minimize the impact of estate and inheritance taxes. If your assets amount to more than $600,000, it's wise to seek the professional services of an attorney, accountant, or financial planner who is familiar with the particulars of your state's inheritance and estate tax laws.

In the absence of a large or complex estate, however, writing a will is not a difficult task. Although wills as we think of them have been around for the past five hundred years, it is only in the past fifty years that lawyers have made themselves "indispensable" to the process.[1]

You *can* write your own will. There are guidebooks and computer software programs to walk you through the process (see "Bibliography and Resources"). Check the Yellow Pages for local "Legal Document Preparation Services."

HEALTH-CARE DIRECTIVES

Health-care directives go by a variety of names, including advance directives, medical directives, living wills, or directives to physicians. All such documents convey your wishes about life-prolonging treatment should you become ill and unable to express yourself. A kind of contract with your physicians, this document binds doctors either to honor your instructions or help transfer your care to others who will. Anyone over the age of eighteen can make a health-care directive, which, like a will, can be changed or revoked at any time.

All branches of Judaism support and encourage the use of

medical directives, or living wills, that are sensitive to Jewish values. The movements publish study guides and living wills, some of which are listed below. Computer programs for writing wills also include health-care directives.

In general, health-care directives describe several specific illness scenarios (e.g., coma, dementia) and possible interventions (e.g., cardiopulmonary resuscitation, artificial nutrition and hydration, pain medication). Some medical directives include alternative choices, with check-off boxes. For example:

If I am in a persistent vegetative state:

❏ I do not wish antibiotics to be administered.
❏ I do wish to be given antibiotics.

Given the complexity of medical technology and the number of possible scenarios, however, there is no way to write a living will that can respond to every situation. That is why people who write medical directives are urged to designate someone to make decisions should they become unable to express their wishes.

Naming a health-care proxy, also called a durable power of attorney, requires a separate document, usually a simple one-page form that must be signed by you, the designated proxy, and witnesses. Proxies tend to be family members, though the responsibility can be assumed by a close friend or your rabbi. Your personal physician cannot, however, act both as your health-care proxy and as your doctor.

Your health-care proxy should be given a copy of the proxy document and also copies of any health-care directives; any "alternative agents" listed on the proxy form should also have a copy.

Most states will honor a directive written in another state, provided it accords with the laws of that state. State laws vary in many ways, including the crucial matter of witnessing.

In order for any health-care directive to be binding and legal, it must be witnessed by two adults and/or notarized according to the particulars of the state. Some states prohibit spouses or physicians from acting as witness; some states do not require a notary's seal. Make sure you know and fulfill all such regulations. Attorneys will be able to provide this kind of information, as will legal clinics. Guidebooks and computer programs for will-writing provide state-by-state lists of regulations.

ORGAN DONATION: Filling out an organ donor card is the simplest of all medical directives, and one that is supported by virtually all rabbinic authorities. The religious precept of *p'kuach nefesh* (the saving of a life) is fulfilled with this *matan chaim,* or gift of life. In the words of Rabbi Isaac Klein, "There can be no greater *kevod hamet* [respect for the dead] than to bring healing to the living."[2]

Becoming an organ donor is easy. Organ donation forms or cards are available from a number of organizations. In most states, you can become a donor by checking off the appropriate box on your driver's license application form and applying an "organ donor" sticker to your license.

It is most important to inform loved ones, your physician, and your rabbi of this decision, and your status as an organ donor should be noted in all health-care directives.

See "Bibliography and Resources."

FINAL ARRANGEMENTS

For most of the Jewish past, people did not need to make "choices" about their own funerals. Everyone knew that the community would prepare their bodies according to Jewish law and bury them among family members in the local Jewish cemetery. Today, of course, most families are scattered, Jews are unfamiliar with traditional practices, and for the most part view Jewish law and custom as advisory rather than binding. Which means that funerals, like all other life-cycle events, present liberal Jews with an array of choices.

The two major elements that can be taken care of in advance of final illness are purchasing a funeral plot and expressing your wishes about funeral arrangements. There is information about these subjects elsewhere in this book; however, there are a few considerations specific to planning for oneself.

Widowed-and-remarried parents should inform their children if they have a preference of where they wish to be buried. Likewise, intermarried couples who want to be buried side by side will do their survivors a great favor if they purchase plots in advance.

It should be noted that an empty plot is not an irrevocable purchase; it can be sold like any other real estate. When families relocate, for example, they frequently sell plots in their old community. Grave sites can be sold (at a premium) by the cemetery itself or a broker, or privately by the owner.

Making "final arrangements" for your own funeral can be as simple as expressing your wishes to loved ones; difficult as this conversation may be, an honest discussion ultimately spares survivors anguish and argument. It's always a good idea to put your preferences in writing. This document can take the form of a letter to family members, or to a rabbi or funeral director.

It is also possible to pay for your own funeral through a "pre-need funeral contract," which can be very specific (right down to the kind of casket and shrouds to be used) or just a more general fund for the family to spend as they see fit.

Pre-need contracts have become a major source of income for funeral homes, which aggressively market them to older adults. However, while there are many reputable mortuaries, some consumer advocates warn against establishing a funeral trust or purchasing a pre-need insurance policy from a funeral home. In addition to the occasional scoundrels, there have been cases where mortuaries simply went out of business, leaving policyholders without funds or recourse. A separate bank account, expressly reserved for funeral and burial expenses, is a safe way to set aside funds and spare family members the expense.

Any method of financing a pre-need contract has tax and Medicaid consequences, which should be considered prior to purchase. If you have questions about a particular contract or plan, ask your financial advisor, accountant, or attorney

Loved ones should be informed about any arrangements, including the location of documents such as a plot deed, funeral insurance policy, bank account, or contract.

ETHICAL WILLS

Leaving a spiritual legacy to family and friends is a time-honored Jewish custom. The tradition cites the beginnings of this practice in the great biblical "charges" of Jacob and Moses, given to their sons and heirs prior to their deaths. In centuries past, rabbis imparted final words of wisdom to their communities, with instructions about the proper way to live a Jewish life.[3] But since the nineteenth century at least, ordinary people have also written about their lives and dreams, leaving a precious legacy to children and grandchildren.[4]

Writing an ethical will challenges you to name what is most important in your life, and how you wish to be remembered. It can also be a way of finishing unfinished business. Of forgiving and seeking forgiveness. Of making sure that your feelings will not be misunderstood. A document at least as important as a living will, an ethical will is a legacy that really does live on, in the hearts and minds of those who read it. Make sure your heirs know that the ethical will exists; keep it with other important documents.

Some synagogues hold an ethical will-writing workshop in the days between Rosh Hashanah and Yom Kippur, traditionally a time of reflection. After explaining the concept and perhaps reading a few examples, participants are given paper and pens. Writing ethical wills with other members of your congregation is a way to accomplish a challenging task within the comfortable embrace of community.

Other "propitious" times for writing an ethical will might be when preparing for a life-cycle event: the birth of a grandchild, a bar or bat mitzvah, or a wedding. Like all other wills, ethical wills can be updated at any time.

There is no standard form for an ethical will. The outline and example that follow are suggestions only; tools to help overcome inertia or writer's block.

1. Opening: Most people think of ethical wills as a letter and begin with a salutation. One way to get started is by

describing the physical setting where you are writing, and then move on to reflect upon how you have come to this moment in your life.

2. Your Journey: Tell your personal history. You might include stories about your parents and siblings, a description of the community in which you grew up, and something about events and people that shaped your life, including how Judaism shaped your journey. The more specific the details, the better.

3. What Counts: What do you believe in? What is most important to you? How has Judaism shaped or informed your beliefs and values?

4. Closing Wishes: What is it you wish to bequeath to your spiritual heirs, who might be children, grandchildren, a spouse, nieces, nephews, friends? Try to be specific in describing your hopes and dreams. Some people spell out their wishes regarding funeral arrangements and mourning. Some end with a prayer.

SAMPLE ETHICAL WILL

Dear Children:

I am sitting in the library at the temple. The date is November 25, 1998, and the sun is shining. I feel calm and happy and healthy as I write, even though I imagine you will be in tears when you read these words. It's been three years since Grandpa Joe died. It's been very hard for me since then, but your support and my memories of him have helped me. And seeing my grandchildren grow into fine young people keeps me feeling young.

When I was a little girl growing up in Brooklyn, it

seemed everyone was Jewish and I didn't have to think about what it meant. My grandparents lived upstairs from us, and I remember hearing them argue sometimes, and hearing them laugh sometimes, too.

When Marcy married Bill, I thought my heart would break. But his conversion showed me that being Jewish isn't a neighborhood or where you come from. It's what you do.

One of the high points of my life was my bat mitzvah, already five years ago. I was 65 years old at the time. It was incredible. Thinking about it makes me cry.

To me, being good to others is the most important thing in life. Being kind, helping people who need help, taking care of your family. These are the key to life, and also I think what it means to be Jewish. To pursue justice is important and to take care of other Jews in the world. Although I was safe in America, the Holocaust is still in my memory. You must not forget what happened then and make sure "never again."

For Marcy and Bill, daughter and son-in-law, I wish you many years together, and to see your grandchildren's bar and bat mitzvahs like me. It is a high point in life, like nothing else.

Ellie and Ari, you are wonderful grandchildren. Be good to your parents and to each other. Be brave and happy. Do something wonderful with your lives; I know you will.

Keep on learning. It keeps you young.

Don't cry too much when I go. My life has been wonderful. I was lucky in my marriage and mostly healthy. I wish the same for all of you.

Bury me simply, like we discussed, according to Jewish tradition. Don't spend money on a fancy stone, either.

Always remember that I love you.

AND DON'T FORGET: It is crucial that documents be stored in a safe location that is known to your loved ones. Give copies of all health-care directives, including the durable power of attorney, to your health-care proxy, other close family members, your primary-care physician, your lawyer, and your rabbi.

Make sure the following information is easily available, too, and if any of this data is stored on a computer, print a hard copy and keep it together with legally executed documents.

- Social Security number, birth date, and place of birth. Mother's maiden name. Your Hebrew name, and your parents' Hebrew names.
- A list of assets, including all bank accounts, brokerage accounts, insurance policies (health, life, house, automobile, etc.), safe deposit boxes.
- Name, phone numbers, and addresses of your attorney, accountant, financial advisors, brokers.
- Combination numbers to any locks or safes. Keys to safety deposit boxes.

GLOSSARY

aleph-bet—name of the Hebrew alphabet; its first two letters.

aliyah—literally, "to go up." In the synagogue, to be called to the Torah, an honor that may include reading from the scroll, chanting the blessings before and after, or standing with the Torah and readers. "Making *aliyah*" refers to moving to the land of Israel.

aninut—"deep sorrow." The period of mourning between death and the funeral.

Aramaic—ancient Semitic language closely related to Hebrew. The Talmud was written in Aramaic.

aron—Hebrew word for "coffin"; literally, "ark."

Ashkenazic—Jews and Jewish culture of Eastern and Central Europe.

aufruf—literally, "called up." Recognition given when people are called up to the Torah on Shabbat, typically related to a life-cycle event.

avel—a mourner after burial.

avelut—"lamenting." The mourning period following the burial, which includes *shloshim* (the following month), and when a parent has died, an entire year.

Baal Shem Tov—Israel ben Eliezer, the founder of Hasidism, the eighteenth-century Jewish mystical revival movement.

Baruch ata Adonai—words that begin Hebrew blessings, most commonly rendered in English as "Blessed art Thou, Lord our God." This book contains a number of alternative translations.

bat—daughter; daughter of, as in *bat mitzvah,* daughter of the commandment. Pronounced *baht.*

B.C.E.—before the Common Era. Jews avoid the Christian designation B.C., which means "before Christ."

bet din—a court (literally, a "house of law") of three rabbis that is convened to witness and give communal sanction to events such as conversions to Judaism.

bikkur holim—the *mitzvah* of visiting the sick, which is incumbent upon all Jews.

b'racha—blessing. Hebrew blessings begin with the phrase *Baruch Ata Adonai Elohenu melech ha-olam.*

bris—Yiddish for *brit,* the most common way of referring to the covenant of circumcision.

brit—covenant.

brit habat—covenant for a daughter.

brit milah—the covenant of circumcision.

bubbe—Yiddish word for "grandma."

cantor—leader of synagogue services trained in Jewish liturgical music.

C.E.—Common Era. Jews avoid A.D., which stands for *anno domini,* or "the year of our lord."

challah—braided loaf of egg bread, traditional for Shabbat, the holidays, and festive occasions.

chazzan—Hebrew for "cantor." *Chazzanit* is the feminine form.

chutzpah—courage, nerve, brass.

Conservative—a religious movement developed in the United States during the twentieth century as a more traditional response to modernity than that offered by Reform Judaism.

daven—pray.

Diaspora—exile. The dwelling of Jews outside the Holy Land.

d'rash—religious insight, often on a text from the Torah.

d'var Torah—literally, "words of Torah"; an explication of a portion of the Torah.

El Malei Rachamim—"God Filled with Compassion," a funeral prayer that is usually chanted or sung in Hebrew while the congregation stands.

erev—"the evening before" the day. Jewish days begin at sunset, not sunrise.

flayshig—meat food, which, according to *kashrut,* or traditional laws governing what Jews eat, may not be mixed with dairy products.

Gan Eden—the Garden of Eden; heaven.

Gehenna—hell.

gemilut hasadim—acts of loving kindness.

gosses—a dying person. Someone whose death is imminent has entered the state of *gesisah.*

halachah—traditional Jewish law contained in the Talmud and its commentaries.

ha-olam ha-bah—the world to come; the afterlife.

ha-olam ha-zeh—the world that is here; this life.

Hasidism—the eighteenth-century Jewish mystical revival movement that stressed God's presence in the world and the idea that joy could be seen as a way of communing with God.

havdalah—separation. The Saturday evening ceremony that separates Shabbat from the rest of the week.

hevra kadisha—burial society. Literally, "holy society."

hoveret—memorial book or pamphlet.

huppah—wedding canopy.

Kabbalah—literally, "receiving" or "that which is received." The name of the Jewish mystical tradition from the twelfth and thirteenth centuries, developed in southern France and Spain. The literary centerpiece of Kabbalah is a book called the Zohar.

Kaddish—the prayer most associated with mourning, a doxology, or listing of God's attributes.

kashrut—traditional system of laws that govern what Jews eat.

kevod ha-met—respect for the dead, literally, for the corpse.

Kiddush—sanctification; also the blessing over wine; also the gathering for wine, bread, and often a light meal after Saturday morning Shabbat services.

kippah—head covering, skullcap; *kippot* is the plural form. The Yiddish word is *yarmulke*.

kohane—the biblical social class that comprised the priesthood of the ancient Temple.

kosher—foods deemed fit for consumption according to the laws of *kashrut*.

k'riah—the ritual tearing of garments prior to a funeral.

levayah—funeral; literally, "accompanying."

Levite—the biblical social class that assisted the priests in the ancient Temple.

ma'ariv—"evening." Also the evening worship service.

matzevah—gravestone.

mazel tov—"Good luck." In common usage, it means "Congratulations."

mensch—person; an honorable, decent person.

Midrash—imaginative exposition of stories based on the Bible.

mikvah—ritual bath.

milchig—dairy foods, which, according to *kashrut,* may not be mixed with meat.

mincha—"afternoon." Also the afternoon worship service.

minyan—a prayer quorum of ten adult Jews.

Mishnah—the first part of the Talmud, comprised of six "orders" of laws regarding everything from agriculture to marriage.

mitzvah—a sacred obligation or commandment. *Mitzvot* is the plural form.

Motzi—a blessing over bread recited before meals.

Mourner's Kaddish—the most commonly recited version of Kaddish; read at funerals and at the end of all worship services.

ner daluk—"burning light," the seven-day candle burned in a *shiva* house.

nichum avelim—comforting the bereaved.

oneg Shabbat—literally, "joy of the Sabbath." A gathering, for food and fellowship, after Friday night synagogue services.

onen—a mourner during the period immediately following the death and prior to the funeral. *Onenim* is the plural form.

Orthodox—in general use, the term refers to Jews who follow traditional Jewish law. The modern Orthodox movement developed in the nineteenth century in response to the Enlightenment and Reform Judaism.

parasha—the weekly Torah portion.

Pesach—Passover.

p'kuach nefesh—the religious principle of preserving life, which is considered so important that other precepts may be violated for its sake.

rabbi—teacher. A rabbi is a seminary-ordained member of the clergy. "The rabbis" refers to the men who codified the Talmud.

Rashi—Rabbi Solomon Ben Isaac, one of the greatest of bible commentators, 1040–1105.

Reconstructionist—a religious movement begun in the United States in the twentieth century by Mordecai Kaplan, who saw Judaism as an evolving religious civilization.

Reform—a movement begun in nineteenth-century Germany that sought to reconcile Jewish tradition with modernity. Reform Judaism does not accept the divine authority of *halachah*.

Rosh Hodesh—first day of every lunar month, a semiholiday.

seudat havra'ah—meal of recuperation or consolation, served in the *shiva* home after the funeral.

Shabbat—Sabbath. In Yiddish, Shabbos.

shacharit—the morning prayer service.

shanah—year. Also the first year of mourning.

Shema—the Jewish prayer that declares God's unity.

shiva—the seven-day period of mourning following the funeral.

shleymut—wholeness. From the same Hebrew root as *shalom.*

shloshim—The thirty-day period following burial, which includes the seven days of shiva.

shtetl—small East European towns inhabited by Ashkenazic Jews before the Holocaust.

shul—synagogue.

Shulchan Aruch—a classic code or guide to Jewish law, *halachah.* Written by Joseph Karo, a sixteenth-century rabbi. The title means "Prepared Table." A source of many laws pertaining to death and mourning.

siddur—prayer book.

simcha—joy and the celebration of joy.

tachrichim—shrouds.

taharat hamishpachah—laws of family purity prescribing women's sexual availability and the use of *mikvah.*

tahor—pure.

tallis, tallit—prayer shawl. *Tallis* is Yiddish; *tallit,* Hebrew.

Talmud—a collection of rabbinic thought and laws, 200 B.C.E. to 500 C.E.

tikkun olam—repairing the world. A fundamental Jewish concept of taking responsibility in and improving the temporal world.

Torah—the first five books of the Hebrew Bible, divided into fifty-four portions that are read aloud and studied in an annual cycle.

tzedakah—righteous giving or action on behalf of the poor; charity.

Viddui—confessional prayer.

yahrzeit—Yiddish for "a year's time." The anniversary of a death.

Yiddish—the language spoken by Ashkenazic Jews, a combination of early German and Hebrew.

Yizkor—a memorial prayer, and the name of the worship service in which the prayer is recited.

Yom Kippur—Day of Atonement, the holiest of the Days of Awe or High Holy Days.

BIBLIOGRAPHY AND
RESOURCES

Hundreds of books about death, grief, and mourning are available, and more are published every year. Some are targeted for specific kinds of losses: spouse, parent, child, sibling, friend. Others address survivors of loss due to suicide, AIDS, or murder. New resources for bereaved children include everything from picture books geared to prereaders, to young adult fiction, to primers for adult caregivers.

Jewish books about death and mourning cover a wide range, too, from question-and-answer pamphlets about burial customs, to workbooks for bereaved children, to scholarly discussions of *halachah*. With a few exceptions, the following list focuses on Jewish resources: books, pamphlets, and organizations.

Jewish Perspectives on Death and Mourning

Mourning and Mitzvah: A Guided Journal for Walking the Mourner's Path Through Grief to Healing by Anne Brener. Jewish Lights Publishing, 1993. A handsome book that makes traditional Jewish thought and writing accessible, though its self-consciously "spiritual" tone and self-help-guided exercises will not appeal to everyone.

Mornings and Mourning: A Kaddish Journal by E. M. Broner. HarperSanFrancisco, 1994. In this memoir written after her father's death, Broner recounts the experience of saying Kaddish prayers in an Orthodox shul.

The Jewish Way in Death and Mourning by Rabbi Maurice Lamm. Jonathan David Publishers, 1969. A groundbreaking book when it was published, Rabbi Lamm's authoritative and thorough treatment remains a popular source, from an Orthodox perspective.

When a Grandparent Dies: A Kid's Own Remembering Workbook for Dealing with Shiva and the Years Beyond by Nechama Liss-Levinson, Ph.D. Jewish Lights Publishing, 1995. For school-aged children, an introduction to Jewish mourning ritual with activities, such as filling in a family tree and assembling a biography of the deceased. Probably most useful when a grandparent dies.

Jewish Insights on Death and Mourning, edited by Jack Riemer. Schocken Books, 1995. A wonderful collection of essays from a wide variety of traditional sources and contemporary writers: rabbis, social workers, physicians, and ordinary Jewish mourners. The brevity of most of these pieces makes it a good book to have in the house during *shiva.*

So That Your Values Live On: Ethical Wills and How to Prepare Them by Jack Riemer and Nathaniel Stampfer. Jewish Lights Publishing, 1991. A collection of ethical wills dating from the 1800s and after, with guidelines and suggestions.

Jewish Views of the Afterlife by Simcha Paull Raphael. Jason Aronson, 1994. A comprehensive overview with much fascinating and unfamiliar source material. Raphael lays out the history of ideas about the afterlife from rabbinic Judaism to Kabbalah to Hasidic tales to a "contemporary psychological model."

Rabbi Rami M. Shapiro, Ph.D., has written three eloquent pamphlets that comfort as they teach: *Open Hands: A Jewish Guide on Dying, Death and Bereavement* (1986); *Open Hearts: A Jewish Guide to Comforting Mourners* (1988), Medic Publishing Co., P.O. Box 89, Redmond, WA 98073-0089 (425-881-2883); and *Last Breaths: A Guide to Easing Another's Dying* (1993). Temple Beth OR P.O. Box 160081, Miami, FL 33116 (305-235-1419).

What Happens After I Die? Jewish Views of Life after Death by Rifat Soncino and Daniel B. Syme. Union of American Hebrew Congregations Press, 1990. The authors cover the major Jewish theories about the afterlife in short, readable form, followed by seven brief essays written by modern Jews—Reform, Conservative, and Orthodox—grappling with the question in a variety of ways.

Healing of Soul, Healing of Body: Spiritual Leaders Unfold the Strength and Solace in Psalms, edited by Rabbi Simkha Y. Weintraub, C.S.W., a project of the Jewish Healing Center. Jewish Lights Publishing, 1994. Jews have looked to Psalms for consolation, comfort, and courage for thousands of years. Rabbis from each of the four contemporary Jewish movements (Conservative, Orthodox, Reconstructionist, and Reform) address ten Psalms that have traditionally been associated with healing.

A Time to Mourn, A Time to Comfort by Dr. Ron Wolfson. The Federation of Jewish Men's Clubs, 1993. A good general guide to Jewish practices and customs, from a Conservative perspective. The book includes many "voices" from the Jewish community, rabbis and lay people, who speak about their own losses and healing.

NONDENOMINATIONAL BOOKS

The National Directory of Bereavement Support Groups and Services (updated annually). ADM Publishing, P.O. Box 751155, Forest Hills, NY 11375-8755 (718-657-1277). This large volume may be found in libraries, and some funeral homes. It is noteworthy for several reasons. It contains an enormous amount and variety of materials, including: recent articles about death, listings of conferences and seminars, state-by-state listings of support groups, and bibliographies that are geared to specific losses, such as "death of a child," "AIDS," "death of a parent," "teenagers." Most important, the directory remains current because it is updated annually.

Talking About Death: A Dialogue Between Parent and Child by Earl A. Grollman. Beacon Press, 1990. Rabbi Grollman, a pioneer in death education for children and author of several books on the subject, here combines a read-along book for young children with a parent's guide. Written for a general, nondenominational audience, it also contains an excellent age-appropriate bibliography.

Empty Arms: Coping After Miscarriage, Stillbirth, and Infant Death by Ilse Shorikee and Arlene Appelbaum. Wintergreen Press, 1992.

When Bad Things Happen to Good People by Rabbi Harold Kushner. Schocken Books, 1989. The now-classic discussion of reconciling the existence of evil and apparently senseless suffering with a belief in God.

A Grief Observed by C. S. Lewis. HarperSanFrancisco, 1994. Deservedly one of the most famous memoirs about loss. Lewis, a devout Catholic, wrote eloquently about his grief and search for meaning after his wife's death.

When Parents Die by Edward Myers. Penguin Books, 1997. A sympathetic guide to the most expected of all losses, which nevertheless can devastate the mourner.

Grieving: How to Go on Living When Someone You Love Dies by Therese A. Rando, Ph.D. D. C. Heath, 1988. A solid general overview of the grieving process, with chapters devoted to the emotional aftermath of different losses, e.g., death of a child, death of a parent, etc.

OTHER PUBLICATIONS AND RESOURCES

Nolo's Simple Will Book by Denis Clifford. Nolo Press, 1989, and accompanying *WillMaker* Software Program. Nolo Press, 1993

United Synagogue Living Will. United Synagogue Book Service, 155 Fifth Avenue, New York, NY 10010 (212-533-8500).

Coalition on Donation, 1100 Boulders Parkway, Suite 500, Richmond, VA 23225 (800-355-SHARE).

Give Me Your Hand: Bikkur Cholim. Traditional and Practical Guidance on Visiting the Sick by Jane Hander Yurow and Kim Hetherington. EKS Publishing, 1029A Solano Avenue, Albany, CA 94706 (510-558-9200). This booklet was based on a symposium held at Adas Israel Congregation in Washington, D.C.

The National Center for Jewish Healing
NCJH focuses on the spiritual needs of Jews living with chronic or acute illness, and provides support for rabbis, chaplains, health-care professionals, and other caregivers through seminars, conferences, and printed materials, which include books of healing prayers.

For more information about the organization and its publications, write or call: National Center for Jewish Healing, c/o JBFCS, 120 West 57th Street, New York, NY 10019 (212-632-4705).

National Institute for Jewish Hospice
Headquartered in Los Angeles and Englewood, New Jersey, the NIJH teaches and trains doctors, nurses, social workers, volunteers, families, rabbis, and Christian clergy in the art of helping the Jewish terminally ill wherever they are: in hospices, nursing homes, or at home.

The twenty-four-hour toll-free number counsels the terminally ill and their family, and helps locate sympathetic physicians, hospices, hospitals, and clergy. The institute is a source of several publications, including *The Jewish Living Will.*

The National Institute for Jewish Hospice
8723 Alden Drive, Suite 148
Los Angeles, CA 90048
(800-446-4448; except in New Jersey,
call 201-816-7324)

Hevra Kadisha
For information about starting a burial society, contact Rabbi Linda Holtzman, director of Practical Rabbinics at the Reconstructionist Rabbinical College. Rabbi Holtzman is a founding member of the Reconstructionist Hevra Kaddisha of Philadelphia and runs workshops and teaches about preparing bodies for burial according to Jewish tradition. She can be reached at the college:
1299 Church Road
Wyncote, PA 19095-1898

The Union of American Hebrew Congregations Committee on Older Adults/Committee on Bio-Ethics
The UAHC produces an impressive list of booklets, brochures, study guides, and case studies dealing with end-of-life issues, death and bereavement, and synagogue support systems. *A Time to Prepare,* for example, is a fifty-three-page workbook that includes advance medical directives, an organ donation form, and several other lists and inventories invaluable to survivors. For a list of publications and order form, write or call Union of American Hebrew Congregations COA/CBE 633 Third Avenue, New York, NY 10017 (212-650-4294).

NOTES

1. Reuven Hammer, *Entering Jewish Prayer* (New York, Schocken Books), pp. 279–281. These two obscure but beautiful prayers are mentioned in the Talmud and Mishnah, but it has been a long time since they have been used. They are unusual for Jewish prayer in that they do not begin by blessing or addressing God but speak directly to the mourner and consoler.

The author changed the translation, adding "our mother Sarah" and changing the plural "our" to "my" to personalize the connection between the reader and the writer.

INTRODUCTION

1. Abraham Joshua Heschel, *The Sabbath* (New York: Farrar, Straus & Giroux, 1951), p. 8.
2. The best guide to Orthodox practice—a groundbreaking book for its time and a primary source for books about Jewish mourning practices ever since—is *The Jewish Way in Death and Mourning* by Rabbi Maurice Lamm (New York: Jonathan David Publishers, 1969).
3. Genesis 2:19. All translations from the Torah, the first five books of the Hebrew Bible, are quoted from *The Five Books of Moses: The Schocken Bible*, Vol. 1, A New Translation with Introductions, Commentary, and Notes by Everett Fox (New York: Schocken Books, 1995).
4. The name for God used in this prayer is Ha-Makom—literally, "the place."

NOTES

1. What Kaddish Means

1. Job 13:15
2. See pages 83–86 for the call-and-response "script."
3. Bernard Lipnick, "A Commentary on the Kaddish," in *Jewish Insights on Death and Mourning,* ed. Jack Riemer (New York: Schocken Books, 1995), pp. 169–172.
4. Rabbi Nosson Scherman, *The Kaddish Prayer* (Brooklyn, N.Y.: Mesorah Publications, 1980), pp. 40–41.
5. For a very comprehensive treatment, see Simcha Paull Raphael, *Jewish Views of the Afterlife* (Northvale, N.J.: Jason Aronson, 1994).
6. Moses Maimonides, *Mishneh Torah,* vol. 1., *The Book of Knowledge,* ed. and trans. Moses Hymanson (Jerusalem: Boys Town Publisher, 1965), p. 91a.

2. Kaddish in Practice

1. Lamm, p. 160.
2. *Encyclopedia Judaica,* vol. 10, pp. 662–663.
3. See n. 8 in chap. 5, "The Funeral," for a translation of the Burial Kaddish.
4. The Rabbi's Kaddish:

Exalted and hallowed be God's greatness
In this world of Your creation.
May Your will be fulfilled
And Your sovereignty revealed
In the days of our lifetime
And the life of the whole house of Israel
Speedily and soon.
And say, Amen.

May You be blessed forever,
Even to all eternity.
May You, most Holy One, be blessed,
Praised and honored, extolled and glorified,
Adored and exalted above all else.
Blessed are You.
Beyond all blessings and hymns, praises and consolations
That may be uttered in this world,
And say, Amen.

Upon Israel, upon the teachers,
Their disciples and all their disciples' disciples,
And upon all those who engage in the study of Torah
Who are here or anywhere else:
May they and you have abundant peace,
Grace, kindness, and mercy,
Long life, ample nourishment, and salvation
From the One Who is in Heaven.
And say, Amen.

May peace abundant descend from heaven
With life for us and for all Israel,
And say, Amen.

May God, Who makes peace on high,
Bring peace to all and to all Israel,
And say, Amen.

5. *Chatzi Kaddish* includes all but the last two lines or sections of the Mourner's Kaddish:

Exalted and hallowed be God's greatness
In this world of Your creation.
May Your will be fulfilled
And Your sovereignty revealed
In the days of our lifetime
And the life of the whole house of Israel
Speedily and soon.
And say, Amen.

May You be blessed forever,
Even to all eternity.
May You, most Holy One, be blessed,
Praised and honored, extolled and glorified,
Adored and exalted above all else.

Blessed are You.
Beyond all blessings and hymns, praises and consolations

That may be uttered in this world,
And say, Amen.

6. The Mourner's Kaddish is substituted at Orthodox funerals on certain days of the year as well. See Lamm.
7. *Encyclopedia Judaica*, vol. 10, p. 661.
8. Bernard Martin, *Prayer in Judaism* (New York: Basic Books, 1968), pp. 148–149. This legend appears in a number of sources, including *Seder Eliyahu Zuta*.
9. The practice of saying Kaddish for eleven rather than twelve months for parents was based on the belief that only evil people spent a full twelve months in Gehenna.
10. Martin, p. 149.
11. On the 1980s series *Northern Exposure*, one whole episode was devoted to pulling together a *minyan* in rural Alaska so the main character, a Jewish doctor from New York City, could recite Kaddish in memory of a beloved uncle. Kaddish was featured on *Thirtysomething* and in made-for-TV movies and documentaries about Judaism and Jewish life.
12. "On Saying Kaddish: A Letter to Haym Peretz, New York, September 16, 1916," *Response* 7, no. 2 (Summer 1973), p. 76.
13. Orthodox women can, if they choose, go to services to say Kaddish, though they are not counted in the required *minyan,* nor should they be audible in their prayers. As Rabbi Lamm puts it, "The daughter, especially if there is no son, may recite the Kaddish quietly to herself." Lamm, p. 167.
14. The tension between Orthodoxy and Jewish women's desire to say Kaddish has been given eloquent voice. For example: See E. M. Broner, *Mornings and Mourning: A Kaddish Journal* (San Francisco: HarperSanFrancisco, 1994); Susan Weidman Schneider, *Jewish and Female* (New York: Simon & Schuster, 1985), pp. 143–147; and Sara Reguer, "Kaddish from the 'Wrong' Side of the Mehitzha," in *On Being a Jewish Feminist,* ed. Susannah Heschel (New York: Schocken Books, 1983), pp. 177–181.

3. CARE OF THE DYING

1. Mishnah, Masehet Semahot, chap. 1, Halachah 1.
2. Ibid., Halachah 5.
3. Ibid., Halachah 4.

4. Ibid., Halachah 4.
5. Ketubot 104a.
6. Isserles in *Shulchan Aruch,* Yoreh Deah 339:1.
7. Ben Sira was the author of *Ecclesiasticus,* a work of poetic maxims.
8. The UAHC publishes pamphlets and study guides about many end-of-life issues, including assisted suicide. See "Bibliography and Resources" for its address.
9. Catholic deathbed confession is now called the "Sacrament of the Sick" rather than "Last Rites."
10. Yoreh Deah 338.
11. Based on the "Confession by the Gravely Ill," *Reform Rabbinical Manual,* p. 108 (New York: Central Conference of American Rabbis, 1988).
12. Reprinted by permission of the translator.
13. Rabbi Rami M. Shapiro, Ph.D., *Last Breaths: A Guide to Easing Another's Dying* (Miami, Fla.: Temple Beth Or, 1993).
14. Lawrence Troster, "Kayla's Prayer," *Conservative Judaism* 37, no. 4 (Summer 1984).

4. HONORING THE DEAD

1. Pirke Avot 4:18.
2. Deuteronomy 21:23.
3. To read extremely moving and detailed first-person accounts of *taharah,* see Debbie Friedman, "Bubby's Last Gift," and Daniel E. Troy, "The Burial Society," in *Jewish Insights on Death and Mourning,* ed. Jack Riemer (New York: Schocken Books, 1995).
4. See Rabbi Margaret Holub, "How Tradition Brought One Community to Life," in Riemer, *Jewish Insights.* Also the video *A Plain Pine Box,* originally a television documentary about a congregational *hevra kadisha* in Minneapolis. There is a book of the same title by Rabbi Arnold Goodman (Hoboken, N.J.: Ktav Publishing House, 1981).
5. Brides go to the *mikvah* before becoming wives. Converts to Judaism immerse as a sign of their change from non-Jew to Jew. According to the *mitzvah* of *taharat hamishpachah*—purification for the sake of the family—women ritually cleanse themselves following their menstrual cycle, and thus change their sexual status from unavailable to available.
6. The pattern of washing is prescribed: the water is ladled over the body,

beginning with the head, then the right front of the body, followed by the left front. The *met* is then raised up so the right and then the left back can be washed.

7. From an Orthodox rabbi's manual, adapted by Rabbi Sue Levi Elwell, Rachel Adler, and Yaffa Weisman, 1991.
8. Ketubot 8b.
9. Semahot 9.
10. Genesis 3:19.
11. Isaac Klein, *A Guide to Jewish Practice* (New York: Jewish Theological Seminary, 1979), p. 275.
12. Genesis 3:19.
13. In biblical references and early rabbinic times, shrouded bodies were buried in caves without any kind of casket. In Israel, it is still common practice to bury the dead directly in the ground, on a bed of reeds, without a coffin.
14. Moed Katan 27a–b.
15. Ecclesiastes Rabbah.

5. THE FUNERAL

1. Genesis 37:34.
2. The use of the pall may have been instituted to discourage expensive caskets.
3. Berakhot 53a.
4. Yoreh Deah 344:1
5. Translation by Rabbi Lawrence Kushner.
6. In Orthodox funerals, principle mourners walk behind the hearse for a block or two, to formally fulfill the mitzvah of *levayah*.
7. *Tzidduk Ha'Din* is read either before or after the body is laid in the grave, depending on the rabbi's custom.

Tzidduk Ha-Din

God The Rock, God's word is perfect, for all God's ways are judgment. A God of faithfulness and without iniquity, just and right is God.

God The Rock, perfect in every work, who can say to God, "What do You do?" God rules below and above. God orders death and restores life. God brings us down to the grave and brings us up again.

God the Rock, perfect in every deed, who can say to God, "What do You do?" You Who speak and act, deal kindly with us, and for the sake of him who was bound like a lamb, listen and act.

Just in all Your ways, O perfect Rock, slow to anger and full of compassion, spare and have pity upon parents and children. Yours is the way of forgiveness and compassion.

You are just, O God, in ordering death and reviving the dead, in your hand is the charge of all spirits. Do not blot out our memory. Let Your eyes regard us with mercy for Yours is the way of forgiveness and compassion. If a man live a year or a thousand years, what profits him? He will be as though he had never been. Blessed is the True Judge, who orders death and revives the dead. Blessed be God, for God's judgment is true, and God's eye discerns all things. God awards man his reckoning and his sentence and all men must acknowledge this.

We know, O God, that Your judgment is righteous; You are justified when You speak and pure when you judge and it is not for us to murmur at your methods. You are Just, O God, and your judgments are righteous.

O true and righteous Judge. Blessed is the true Judge, whose judgments are righteous and true.

The soul of every living thing is in your hand; your might is full of righteousness. Have mercy upon the remnant of the flock in your hands and say unto the destroying angel, "Stay your hand."

You are great in wisdom and mighty in deed. Your eyes are open upon all the ways of the sons of man, to give everyone according to his ways and according to the work of his hand. Declare that God is righteous. God is my Rock and there is only righteousness in God. The Lord gives and the Lord takes. Blessed is the name of the Lord.

God being merciful, forgives iniquity, and does not destroy us. Yea, many times has God turned God's anger away, containing all of God's wrath.

8. THE BURIAL KADDISH
May His great Name be exalted and sanctified,
in the world which will be renewed,
And where He will resuscitate the dead
and raise them up to eternal life,
And rebuild the city of Jerusalem
and complete His Temple within it,

And uproot alien worship from the earth,
and return the service of Heaven to its place,
And where the Holy One, Blessed be He,
    will reign in His sovereignty and splendor.

During your life and during your days,
and during the life of the entire house of Israel
Swiftly and soon.
Amen.

May His great Name be blessed forever and ever.
Blessed, lauded, glorified, extolled,
    upraised, honored, elevated, and praised
Be the Name of the Holy One,
Blessed be He.

Beyond all blessings, songs, praises, and consolations
    that are uttered on earth.
Amen.

May there be abundant peace from Heaven,
    and life upon us and upon all Israel.
Amen.

He Who makes peace in His heights,
May He make peace upon us and upon all Israel.
Amen.

6. THE LANDSCAPE OF MOURNING

1. Elisabeth Kübler-Ross, *On Death and Dying* (New York: Macmillan Publishing Co., 1969).
2. Moed Katan 27b.
3. Lamm, p. 85. Of course, the legal exemption does nothing to assuage a mourner's guilt at "disobeying" a deathbed wish.
4. Funeral directors used to have a rather unsavory reputation because of the unscrupulous dealings of those who misrepresented the law and pushed

expensive services and products on people who were in terrible distress. The abuses of the funeral business were exposed in Jessica Mitford's 1963 book *The American Way of Death,* which led to a public outcry and national regulation of the industry.

5. See the film and book *A Plain Pine Box.*

6. Healing services in nonfundamentalist Christian churches take a similar approach, seeking to foster the healing of the spirit.

7. *A Leader's Guide to Services and Prayers of Healing* is one of several publications made available by the National Center for Jewish Healing, c/o JBFCS, 120 West 57th St., New York, NY 10019 (212-632-4705).

8. Midrash, Genesis Rabbah 27:7.

7. *SHIVA:* THE SEVEN DAYS

1. Genesis 50:10.

2. After the third day, *halachah* makes more exceptions to the laws against working, though in fairly extraordinary circumstances, such as when there might be a hardship to the individual or the community. Lamm, pp. 116–120.

3. Proverbs 20:27.

4. Yoreh Deah 378:1.

5. Mazon supports soup kitchens, food pantries, and other programs that serve both Jews and non-Jews, in the United States and around the world. Mazon, 12401 Wilshire Boulevard, Suite 303, Los Angeles, CA 90025-1015 (mazonmail@aol.com).

6. The list of don'ts is extensive and much debated. The prohibition against bathing, which at one point was a great luxury, is now generally interpreted as "Don't soak in the tub but a quick shower is permitted." *Shiva* was not intended to create hardship for mourners; *halachah* sets forth all kinds of exceptions to the prohibitions. Lamm, pp. 111–120.

7. Prayers and psalms of praise and joy tend to be omitted out of respect for the bereaved. Lamm, pp. 104–108.

8. Abraham Joshua Heschel, *The Sabbath* (New York: Farrar, Straus & Giroux, 1995).

9. For a more detailed discussion of how *shiva* is affected by holidays, see Lamm, pp. 94–97.

10. A resource for school-age children during *shiva* is: Nechama Liss-

Levinson, *When a Grandparent Dies: A Kid's Own Remembering Workbook for Dealing with Shiva and the Year Beyond* (Woodstock, Vt.: Jewish Lights Publishing, 1995).

11. In the past, walking around the block may have been a way of escorting the soul of the dead who lingered during *shiva,* allowing it to finally ascend.

12. Anne Brener, *Mourning and Mitzvah* (Woodstock, Vt.: Jewish Lights Publishing, 1993), p. 104.

13. Alisa Rubin Kurshan, "Knitting Up the Tear," in *Jewish Insights on Death and Mourning,* ed. Jack Riemer (New York: Schocken Books, 1995), p. 167. This essay contains a more complete version of this ceremony.

    "While the Psalm will conjure up the memory of the funeral it is also most appropriate this time. After having walked in the valley of the shadow of death, the mourners must seek new sources of comfort and strength."

14. Ezekiel 24:17. And in Job 3:13, Job's friends sit on the ground with him for seven days, saying nothing, "for they saw how very great his suffering was."

15. Ecclesiastes 7:2.

16. Some rabbis like to say that a week spent sitting *shiva* saves years on the psychiatrist's couch later.

8. THE FIRST YEAR

1. Yoreh Deah 394.

2. Lamm, p. 185. Although principal mourners are not supposed to marry during the thirty days, the rule is set aside if preparations have already been made and postponement would present a financial burden.

3. Rabbi Solomon ben Isaac (1040–1105), known as "Rashi," was one of the greatest of bible commentators.

4. In liberal congregations, both women and men are counted in this quorum. Orthodox and some very traditional Conservative *minyans* do not count women.

5. See E. M. Broner, *Mornings and Mourning: A Kaddish Journal* (San Francisco: HarperSanFrancisco, 1994).

6. Roberta Leviton, "Minyan and Memory," *Hadassah Magazine,* November 1994, p. 18.

7. Arthur Gross Schaefer, "A Way to Mark Shloshim," in Riemer, pp. 191–194.

8. Yoreh Deah 394.

9. Semachot.

10. Jews have straddled the two calendars—secular and sacred, lunar and

solar—for two thousand years. The Hebrew calendar months are made up
of either 29 or 30 days, which add up to a 354-day year, which is 11.25 days
short of a solar year. The discrepancy is corrected with the addition of a leap
month every few years. For a more general discussion of "Jewish time" and
the calendar, see *Living a Jewish Life* by Anita Diamant (New York:
HarperCollins, 1991), pp. 167–169.

11. Exodus 20:12.

12. Leviton, p. 19.

13. Rabbi Moses ben Israel Isserles (1525–1572), a Polish scholar best remembered for his seminal work, the *Mappah* ("tablecloth") which sought to uni-
versalize the *Shulchan Aruch* ("set table") by adding Ashkenazic usage to the
Sephardic practices it described.

14. With thanks to Rabbi Carl Perkins.

15. Anne Brener, "Approaching Yahrzeit," *Sh'ma: A Journal of Jewish Responsibility* 27, no. 534 (May 16, 1997; 9 Iyar 5757), pp. 6–7.

16. The seven-day holiday of Sukkot is immediately followed by the holiday of
Shemini Atzeret.

17. Given the nature of the lunar year, the Hebrew calendar includes an occa-
sional leap month, a second Adar, which is called Adar II or Adar Sheni.
Generally, deaths that occur during Adar II in a leap year are observed in
Adar on regular years and in Adar II in leap years.

18. A short service for lighting a memorial candle is found in *Kol Haneshamah:
Songs, Blessings and Rituals for the Home* (Wyncote, Pa.: Reconstructionist
Press, 1991), pp. 136–137.

9. The Consolations of Memory

1. This poem appears in *Vetaher Libeynu* (Purify Our Hearts), *siddur* of Congregation Beth El of the Sudbury River Valley (Sudbury, Mass., 1980), p.
114. It appears here by permission of the author.

2. Jacob and Laban built a *matzevah* to witness their truce and mark a boundary between them (Genesis 31:43–47). And Jacob built a pillar at the place he
called Beth El (House of God), where he had his famous vision of the ladder (Genesis 28:18). The first biblical mention of a burial pillar appears in
Genesis 35:20: "Yaakov set up a standing-pillar over the burial-place, that is
Rahel's burial pillar of today."

3. Lamm, p. 189.

4. "People used to bring out the deceased for burial: the rich on a tall state bed,

ornamented and covered with rich coverlets, the poor on a plain bier. And the poor felt ashamed. Therefore a law was established that all should be brought out on a plain bier." Moed Katan 27a–b.

5. In Talmudic times, when bodies were buried in caves, the practice was to retrieve the bones after about a year, and then to prepare them for permanent interment.

6. Based on a ceremony compiled by Howard Cooper.

7. Used by permission of the author.

8. Isaac Klein, *A Guide to Jewish Religious Practice* (New York: Jewish Theological Society, 1979), p. 300.

9. There is some dispute about Purim and Rosh Hodesh, the celebration of the New Moon. See Klein, p. 300.

10. Those who visit in the first month should be prepared for what they will see. The grave will probably not be planted and may look very raw.

11. Dr. Ron Wolfson, *A Time to Mourn, A Time to Comfort* (New York: Federation of Jewish Men's Clubs, 1993), p. 242.

12. Psalm 103:15 continues:

he blooms like a flower of the field:

a wind passes by and it is no more,
its own place no longer knows it.
But the Lord's steadfast love is for all eternity.

13. Riemer, pp. 129–130. See also David J. Wolpe's essay, in Riemer, "Why Stones Instead of Flowers?"

14. From Barry Freundel's essay "Yizkor: The Unending Conversation," in Riemer, p. 198.

15. Some rabbinic authorities excused mourners from Yizkor to spare them the pain it might cause, but *halachah* comes down on the side of saying it even during the first week. See Rabbi Chaim Binyamin Goldberg, *Mourning in Halachah: The Laws and Customs of the Year of Mourning* (New York: Mesorah Publications, 1991), pp. 405–406.

16. The reason these three Yizkor services were added is usually explained by the fact that *tzedakah* is mentioned in the holiday liturgies.

17. See "Yizkor, Yahrzeit, and the Cycle of Seasons" in Brener, for her discussion of the spiritual "tasks" involved at each of these points along the first year's cycle.

18. Bava Batra 9a.

19. The word *tzedakah* is usually translated as "charity." However, the word "charity" is based on the Latin *caritas,* which means Christian love. *Tzedakah* is derived from the Hebrew word *tzedek,* which means "justice."

20. Brener, p. 180.

21. Proverbs 10:2. Bava Batra 10a. Midrash makes the same point, though in even more dramatic terms:

> *A man in the habit of giving charity was drowned at sea. When he reappeared among his friends and was asked, "Are you not the one who was lost at sea?" the pious man explained the miracle of his presence. "When I went down to the nethermost depths, I heard a mighty roaring among the waves. One wave called out to another, 'We must rush to bring this man up from the sea because he dispensed charity all his days.'"* [Avot de Rabbi Natan 3]

22. Based on Danny Siegel's "19 Occasions for Giving Tzedakah" in Danny Siegel, *Gym Shoes and Irises: Personalized Tzedakah* (Spring Valley, N.Y.: Town House Press, 1982), p. 70.

23. Baba Batra 9a.

24. Sota 14a, Eruvin 18a, Shabbat 127a–b. See Siegel, "A Study Guide to Tzedakah," pp. 119–127.

25. Sota 14a.

26. According to Maimonides' "ladder of tzedakah," which ranked the merits of various forms of charitable giving, the highest form is that which is given anonymously and permits another to become self-sufficient.

27. Sephardic Jews name babies after living relatives. For more about Jewish baby-naming customs, see Anita Diamant, *The New Jewish Baby Book* (Woodstock, Vt.: Jewish Lights Publishing, 1993), pp. 15–84.

10. PARTICULAR LOSSES

1. Funeral homes sometimes provide workbooks for children. Also, see "Bibliography and Resources."

2. With thanks to David Browning, M.S.W., whose thoughtful comments inform this section, and much of this book.

3. Lamm, p. 170.

4. For more about the history of conversion, see Anita Diamant, *Choosing a Jewish Life: A Handbook for People Converting to Judaism and for their Family and Friends* (New York: Schocken Books, 1997).

5. For more about *halachic*-Orthodox views on this question, see Maurice Lamm, *Becoming a Jew,* (Middle Village, N.Y.: Jonathan David Publishers, 1991), pp. 248–250.

6. *Halachah* prohibits Jews from attending any non-Jewish religious service, even the funeral of a parent or sibling. However, the tradition is even more emphatic about going beyond the "letter of the law" regarding converts. See Mishnah, Sheviit 10:9

7. © Hilary Tham; reprinted by permission. From *Bad Names for Women* (Washington, D.C.: Word Works, 1992).

8. Rebecca T. Alpert, *Confronting Mortality and Facing Grief: Jewish Perspectives on Death and Mourning* (Wyncote, Pa.: Reconstructionist Rabbinical College, 1997), p. 11.

9. *Shulchan Aruch,* Yoreh Deah, 374:8.

10. Reconstructionist Rabbinical Association, *Rabbi's Manual* (Wyncote, Pa.: Reconstructionist Rabbinical Association, 1997), p. D-28. Adapted from a prayer by Rabbi Sandy Eisenberg Sasso. This is also listed as a prayer to be used on the occasion of a miscarriage with the following notes: "When used on the occasion of a miscarriage, this prayer is to be recited privately or among friends, soon after the miscarriage, or to coincide with the time when the period of mourning following what would have been childbirth might naturally be concluded.

"When used for a stillbirth, it is to be recited privately or among friends, soon after the stillbirth.

"Though tragic events both, a stillbirth and miscarriage cannot be equated, and the experience of grief in these two cases should not be treated as the same. Nonetheless, we believe that this prayer is appropriate in both circumstances."

11. For example, the barrenness of Sarah, Hannah, and Rachel, who at one point cries out, "Give me children, lest I die" (Genesis 30:1).

12. Klein, p. 282.

13. Ibid., p. 283.

14. There may still be some Jewish cemeteries that segregate the graves of suicides; however, they would be exceptions.

15. The Union of American Hebrew Congregations produces a pamphlet called *Assisted Suicide,* which may be ordered from the address listed in the Bibliography.

NOTES

PART IV: EIGHT WAYS TO SAY KADDISH
TRANSLATIONS, INTERPRETATIONS, AND REFLECTIONS

1. © Everett Fox; used by permission. Everett Fox is Allen M. Glick Professor of Judaic and Biblical Studies at Clark University. He is the translator of *The Five Books of Moses* (New York: Schocken Books, 1995), for which he also wrote the notes and commentary. Professor Fox notes: "In all of Jewish prayer, no other passage has the rhythmic drive of what Max Lerner called 'the thunderous syllables of the Kaddish.' It is as close as rabbinic prayer gets to rhyme—and this is not accidental. The reciting of the Kaddish in a moment of personal pain is a soothing act, and this is facilitated not only by the fact that the prayer is said in public, i.e., with the loving support of the community, but by the very sounds of the prayer itself. Like a mantra in Eastern religions, the repeating sounds of the Kaddish serve to create a mood and a place into which one can fit one's emotions.

   "Because of this aspect of the prayer, it is important for the translator to echo the Aramaic wherever possible. The sequences, 'magnified . . . sanctified,' 'willed . . . fulfilled,' 'words-of-praise . . . words-of-song / words-of-blessing, and words-of-comfort,' are designed to echo the effect of the original, and to allow the reciter to enter a rhythmic world where healing can begin to take place. Similarly, the long sequence of 'may it be ____' is meant, despite the obvious lack of elegant verbs for 'praise' in English, to draw the reader toward God's name and, eventually, toward the goal of all prayer: peace for ourselves and peace for the world.

   "I would like to thank Professor Edward Greenstein for his suggestions regarding this translation."

   Professor Fox has written two versions of the Orphan's Kaddish. The author elected to include only the gender-neutral version, which substitutes "God" for masculine pronouns "He" and "His."

2. Rabbi Jules Harlow, ed., *Machzor for Rosh Hashanah and Yom Kippur* (New York: Rabbinical Assembly, 1978); used by permission.

3. Translation from *Vetaher Libeynu* (Purify Our Hearts), the prayer book of Congregation Beth El of the Sudbury River Valley (Sudbury, Mass., 1980), p. 118.

4. © Marge Piercy; used by permission.

5. © Hyman Plutzik; used by permission. Hyman Plutzik, *The Collected Poems* (Brockport, N.Y.: Boa Editions, 1987), p. 270.

6. © Samuel Yosef Agnon, *Kol Seporav*, vol. 4 (Tel Aviv: Schocken Books, 1955), pp. 288–289. The ancient image of God reviewing His "troops" comes

from the Mishnah (Mo'ed, Rosh Hashanah 1:2) and is echoed in the Yom Kippur prayer *U'Netaneh Tokef.* The poem was commissioned in memory of soldiers killed in Israel's War of Independence.

7. © Debra Cash; used by permission. Ms. Cash notes: "The traditional text of the Kaddish affirms the Supremacy of God in the face of mortality. Yet the individual gesture of the mourner standing among the congregation says 'I have suffered. I am alone in my unique loss. Be with me in order to make it bearable.'

"I decided to take the radical turn of writing a Kaddish that did not mention God, yet that could have the flow and clarity of liturgical language, the formulaic quality that would make it possible to say such words every day for eleven months. It also seemed necessary to encompass the different types of feelings that would wash over an individual in the course of a year of mourning and might mark different emotional landmarks in that process."

8. © Marcia Falk; used by permission.

APPENDIX: PLANNING FOR THE UNTHINKABLE

1. Barbara Kate Repa, Stephen Elias, and Ralph Warner, *WillMaker* (Berkeley, Calif.: Nolo Press, 1994), p. 1/6.

2. Klein, p. 275.

3. Jack Riemer and Nathaniel Stampfer, *So That Your Values Live On: Ethical Wills and How to Prepare Them* (Woodstock, Vt.: Jewish Lights Publishing, 1991). See the ethical will of Moshe Yehoshua Zelig Hakoen, head of a Latvian rabbinic court (c. 1790–1855), pp. 10–18.

4. In Riemer and Stampfer, see the ethical will of Rose Weiss Baygel, an immigrant from Riga who worked in a sweatshop, picketed with the Garment Workers Union, and raised three children, pp. xxiv–xxv.

INDEX

Anita Diamant is the author of *Choosing a Jewish Life*, *The New Jewish Wedding*, *Living a Jewish Life*, *The New Jewish Baby Book*, *Bible Baby Names*, and a novel, *The Red Tent*. She is a former columnist for the *Boston Globe Magazine*, and her articles have also appeared in *Parenting Magazine*, *Parents*, *McCall's*, *Reform Judaism*, and *Hadassah Magazine*. She lives in Newton, Massachusetts, with her husband and daughter.